The Tale of Gamelyn: From the Harleian Ms. No. 7334, Collated with Six Other Mss

Anonymous

Clarendon Press Series

THE TALE OF GAMELYN

SKEAT

a

𝕷𝖔𝖓𝖉𝖔𝖓

HENRY FROWDE

OXFORD UNIVERSITY PRESS WAREHOUSE
AMEN CORNER, E.C.

𝕹𝖊𝖜 𝖄𝖔𝖗𝖐

MACMILLAN & CO., 66 FIFTH AVENUE

Clarendon Press Series

THE

TALE OF GAMELYN

FROM THE HARLEIAN MS. No. 7334, COLLATED
WITH SIX OTHER MSS.

EDITED

WITH NOTES AND A GLOSSARIAL INDEX

BY THE

Rev. WALTER W. SKEAT, Litt. D.

ELRINGTON AND BOSWORTH PROFESSOR OF ANGLO-SAXON, AND
FELLOW OF CHRIST'S COLLEGE, CAMBRIDGE

SECOND EDITION, REVISED

Oxford

AT THE CLARENDON PRESS

M DCCC XCIII

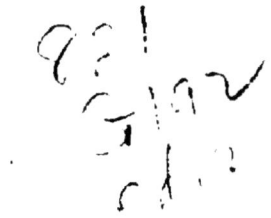

566116

Oxford
PRINTED AT THE CLARENDON PRESS
BY HORACE HART, PRINTER TO THE UNIVERSITY

CONTENTS.

INTRODUCTION.

§ 1. AMONGST the numerous Middle-English poems by anonymous authors which have come down to us, The Tale of Gamelyn is worthy of particular attention for several reasons. In the first place, it is a good example of the kind of story which was at one time very popular. It is, essentially, a *lay*, i. e. an older and longer kind of ballad, and has a certain connection with the famous set of ballads relating to Robin Hood. In the second place, it is a good example of the Middle-English of the fourteenth century, and exhibits a dialect not far removed from that which, in process of time, has become the standard literary language. Lastly, it has an additional interest on account of its peculiar connection with our two greatest poets, Chaucer and Shakespeare. The nature of this connection will be discussed presently.

§ 2. I am not aware that the original of the present version of the Tale can be precisely pointed out. · Stories which relate the fate of a younger brother who is deprived of his inheritance by the jealousy of a senior brother, and who nevertheless achieves great prosperity, are as old as the time of Joseph. If there is anything peculiar in the present tale, it is that the second brother takes part with the younger rather than with the elder; for popular stories usually represent the youngest of three sons as being the only one who comes to any good. I should be inclined to believe that the tale is not the invention of its author, but was derived, like the Lay of Havelok, from a Scandinavian original, of which there may have existed an Anglo-French version.

The names which occur in it are very few, but are worth a moment's consideration. The father of the three sons is called Sir Johan of Boundes, but there is nothing to indicate the locality of the place so named. In fact, Boundes is probably merely the plural of *bound*, so that the name is equivalent to

Sir John of the Marches or of the Border-land, and we hence obtain no information except that *bound* is a word of pure French origin, from the Old French *bonne*, a limit[1]. It is true that one MS. in the Cambridge University Library (marked Ii. 3. 26) has the reading *burdeuxs*, i. e. Bourdeaux; but this must have been due to the substitution by the scribe of a familiar for an unfamiliar name. The three sons are named Johan, Ote, and Gamelyn. Of these, Johan or John, though ultimately Hebrew, is practically French; we can all remember King John. Ote also appears elsewhere as Otes; see note to l. 727, on p. 46. It is clearly a nominative form of Otoun, the name of a French knight vanquished by the famous Guy of Warwick; and Otoun is merely the French form of Othonem, the accusative of the Latin Otho (cf. G. Otto). The only other names are those of the third son Gamelyn, and of Adam, the 'spencer' or steward of the household. In connection with the latter of these, it is worth remarking that Adam Bell was a famous outlaw. The name of Gamelyn is worthy of more particular examination, because it is here that we have a trace of Scandinavian influence and, at the same time, a point of contact with the ballads that concern Robin Hood.

§ 3. The name Gamelyn can hardly be other than *gamel-īn*, formed with the diminutive suffix *-īn* (as seen in Lat. *Paul-in-us*, *Iust-in-us*) · from the adjective *gamel*, i. e. old. Of course this *gamel*, when used as a personal name, was a mere nickname, and lost its real sense; and the same is true of Gamelyn; but we may fancifully see in it a certain fitness, as I venture to point out below. The word *gamel*, old (also spelt *gamol*, *gomel*, *gomol*), occurs occasionally in Anglo-Saxon poetry, but is, strictly, a Scandinavian form. The word for 'old,' in Icelandic, is invariably *gamall*[2]; in Swedish, *gammall*; and in Danish, *gammel*. The name is extremely appropriate, because Gamelyn is evidently considered

---

[1] There is a place called Bons in Normandy, between Falaise and Caen; but I do not know the meaning of the name.

[2] The form *aldinn* occurs in old poems, as shewn by the examples given in Egilsson's Lexicon Poeticum; but it was never very common, and is now obsolete.

as being the son of his father's old age[1], and considerably younger than his brothers[2]. It is remarkable that the name is still in use; I find the spellings Gamlin and Gamlen in the London Directory for 1884, and the latter form appears in the Clergy Directory and over a shop-door in Cambridge. It may also be assumed to form a part of the word Gamlingay, which is the name of a village between Cambridge and Bedford. It is further interesting as indicating a connection between our tale and the part of England most subject to Scandinavian influence; in other words, it concerns the *Eastern*, not the Western portion, of our island.

§ 4. It can hardly be doubted that the name *Gandeleyn* which occurs in a ballad entitled 'Robyn and Gandeleyn' is a mere corruption of Gamelyn. In the present tale, Gamelyn becomes an outlaw, lives in the wood, and is made master over all the outlaws under the king of the outlaws himself (l. 686). In the ballad[3], we have a very remarkable account, quite different from the usual one, of the death of Robin Hood, who is shot by a certain Wrennok of Doune. Gandeleyn, who calls Robin Hood his 'mayster,' encounters Wrennok, and challenges him to a trial of skill in archery :—

> 'Qwerat xal our marke be?'
>   Seyde Gandeleyn:
> 'Eueryche at otheris herte,'
>   Seyde Wrennok ageyn—

an answer of intense significance. Thereupon Wrennok discharges his arrow, but it passes harmlessly between Gandeleyn's legs, who at once shoots Wrennok through the heart, exclaiming :—

> 'Now xalt thu neuer ʒelpe[4], Wrennok,
>   At wyn ne at ale
> That thou hast slawe goode Robyn
>   And Gandeleyn his knave[5].'

---

[1] Genesis xxxvii. 3.

[2] Hence the epithet 'the *yonge* Gamelyn' is of constant occurrence.

[3] Printed in Ritson, Ancient Songs and Ballads, i. 81; and in Child's English and Scotch Ballads, v. 38. I have used the latter copy.

[4] I.e. boast (A.S. *gilpan*).   [5] Servant; lit. boy.

But this is not the only example of the name's occurrence. It is quite clear that the *Young Gamwell* in the Ballad of Robin Hood and the Stranger is the *Young Gamelyn* of our tale. This remarkable ballad tells of a fight with swords between Robin Hood and a stranger. The stranger wounds Robin, who thereupon demands his name.

> The stranger then answer'd bold Robin Hood,
>   'Ile tell thee where I do dwell;
> In Maxwell town I was bred and born,
>   My name is *young Gamwell.*
>
> For killing of my own father's steward
>   I am forc'd to this English wood,
> And for to seek an uncle of mine,
>   Some call him Robin Hood.'
>
> 'But art thou a cousin of Robin Hood then?
>   The sooner we should have done.'
> 'As I hope to be saved,' the stranger then said,
>   'I am his own sister's son.'

Hereupon they become excellent friends; and Robin Hood tells Little John that he will make young Gamwell one of the crew, saying :—

> 'But he shall be a bold yeoman of mine,
>   *My chief man next to thee.*'

Young Gamwell then takes the name of Will Scadlock; so that Gamelyn is thus curiously identified with the Will Scath-lock, Scadlock, or Scarlet, whose name is tolerably familiar to all who have heard of his more famous master. The sequel of the ballad is somewhat curious. Robin Hood, Little John, and Will Scadlock (as he is now called) go to London to rescue a certain princess, and are matched to fight against three giants, whom they of course slay. The princess is married to Young Gamwell, whom the Earl of Maxfield (not Maxwell, as before) recognises as his lost son. It is easy to see how the same general ideas can be infinitely varied by ballad-writers who had a clear licence to introduce any details which their imaginations could suggest. The Scottish reference to Maxwellton is not happy, and indicates a late date.

§ 5. The most remarkable point is, perhaps, that the 'master outlaw' in the tale of Gamelyn is left unnamed. This is a mark of a somewhat early date. Professor Child well remarks that 'no mention is ever made of him [Robin Hood] in literature before the latter half of the reign of Edward III.' In fact, the earliest notice of him is in the B-text (*second* version) of Piers the Plowman (Pass. v. l. 402), which cannot be earlier than about A. D. 1377.

Even more curious than the absence of name for the outlaw, is the absence of any indication of locality. In these days, we at once associate the outlaw with Sherwood Forest[1]; and the ballad of Robin Hode and Queen Katherine represents Robin Hood as saying :—

> 'I will not leave my bold outlawes
>   for all the gold in Christentie;
> in merry Sherwood Ile take my end,
>   vnder my trusty tree.'
>
> Percy Folio MS., ed. Hales and Furnivall, i. 45.

When Robin Hood has a difficulty with a sheriff, it is usually the sheriff of Nottingham. The fact that The Tale of Gamelyn introduces us to a nameless king of outlaws living in a nameless wood is an indication, as far as it goes, of early date, and suggests that the ballads are indebted to the Tale rather than the converse.

§ 6. Again, the introduction of the wrestling-match, in which Gamelyn vanquishes the champion, reminds us of Havelok's feat in 'putting the stone' twelve feet further than all the other 'champions[2].' The marvellous way in which Gamelyn lays about him, at one time with a 'pestle' (l. 128) and at another with a 'cart-staff' (l. 500), reminds us of Havelok's feat in killing twenty men with the bar of a door (Havelok, ll. 1794—1859). It is highly probable that the author of the Tale was acquainted with the Lay of Havelok, which is clearly connected

[1] 'And *my whole* in merry Sherwood
       Sent, with preter-human luck,
     Missiles, not of steel but fir-wood,
       Through the two-mile-distant buck.'
                    Charade on *Out-law*; by C. S. C.
[2] The Lay of Havelok the Dane, ed. Skeat (E. E. T. S.), l. 1052.

with Lincolnshire.   This furnishes a faint indication of the part
of England to which the Tale possibly belongs.

Another hint is to be obtained from the Vocabulary.   The
number of words of Scandinavian origin are but few ; the chief
are :—a-twynne, 317 ; awe, *s.* 543 ; bone, boone, 149, 153 ; caste, 237,
245 ; cast, *s.* 248 ; deyde, 68 ; felaw, 227, 276, 571, *pl.* 811 ; ferd,
854 ; lawe, 544 ; litheth, 1 ; loft, 127 ; nyggoun, 323 ; rape, *adj.*
101 ; raply, rapely, 219, 424 ; rewthe, 508 ; reysed, 162 ; serk,
259 ; skeet, 187 ; weyuen, 880.   Some of these occur in Chaucer,
viz. a-twynne, bone, caste, deyde, felaw, lawe, rape (but only as
a sb.), rewthe, reyse, weyued, but there is a small residue of
words that indicate a more Northern dialect.   Thus *awe* occurs
in Wyclif, Hampole, Robert of Brunne, the Towneley Mysteries,
the Ormulum, Havelok, Wallace, and the Bruce ; the *Southern*
form being *eye* (A.S. *ege*) which, curiously enough, *also* occurs
in our poem.   *Lithe,* to listen, occurs at least five times ; but
I do not find it in Chaucer.   *Loft* occurs as a substantive, and
is explained in the Promptorium Parvulorum as being equivalent to *soler,* from the Latin *solarium* [1].   *Nyggoun* is only
known to occur here, and in Robert of Brunne's Handlyng
Synne, ll. 5340, 5578, where it is spelt *nygun.*   *Serk* is the
well-known Northern *sark* ; and *skeet* occurs in the Ormulum,
the Northern version of Alexander, Havelok, Sir Gawain, &c.
The scarcity of Scandinavian words is easily accounted for by
the shortness of the poem.

I must not omit to observe here that (as was kindly pointed
out to me by Mr. Kington Oliphant) a certain line in Gamelyn
which occurs twice over (see ll. 277, 764) is quoted almost exactly
from A Poem on the Times of Edward II.   This poem exists in
two copies which differ considerably ; one of these was printed
by Mr. Wright for the Camden Society in 1839, in the volume
entitled Political Songs (pp. 323–345), from 'the Auchinleck MS.
written in the beginning of the reign of Edward III' ; the other
was printed by the Rev. C. Hardwick for the Percy Society in
1849, from the MS. preserved in St. Peter's College, Cambridge.
I refer to the former of these editions, in which l. 475 runs thus :—

---

[1] The substantival use is rare ; the derived adverb *a-lofte* is common,
both in Chaucer and other authors.

'But bi seint Jame of Galice, that many man hath souht.'

I have little doubt that the author of Gamelyn was acquainted with this poem, and it is interesting to note a few further points of resemblance. Thus the expression *in the fen* (Gamelyn, 588) may be illustrated by ll. 142, 143 of the Poem, which stand thus :—

'The porter hath comaundement to hold hem widoute the gate
in the fen.'

The expression *so brouke I*, so common in Gamelyn (ll. 273, 297, 334, 407, 489, 567), occurs in the Poem, l. 187 :—

'For als ich euere brouke min hod vnder min hat.'

The expression *euel mot he the* (Gam. 363) occurs in the Poem, l. 232. The expression *had doon a sory rees* (Gam. 547) may be compared with 'and maken there her res' in the Poem, l. 248 ; cf. also l. 434. The expression *Cristes curs mot thou have* (Gam. 114, 116) is just like that in the Poem, l. 310—'Godes curs moten hii haue.' Other phrases and words occurring in the Poem are *par seinte charite*, l. 128 (misused for *pour sainte charite*) ; *muchele schrewes*, l. 406 ; *for feerd* (=*ferd*), l. 17 ; *god chep*, l. 405 ; *barre* (of justice), l. 343 ; *haluendel*, l. 316 ; *gamen*, l. 367 ; *mot-halle*, l. 292. See also the note to Gamelyn, l. 871. Such phrases and words are not particularly uncommon, but the actual coincidence of a whole line is remarkable ; and we may safely conclude that Gamelyn was written after (but probably not long after) this Poem, which Mr. Hardwick says 'may be fairly assigned to somewhere about the year 1320.'

§ 7. We will now consider the incidental connection of the Tale with the poet Chaucer. It so happens that all the copies of it which have been preserved occur in MSS. of the Canterbury Tales, but it is by no means found in all of them. In three of the best MSS., viz. the Ellesmere MS., the Hengwrt MS., and the Cambridge MS. marked Gg. 4. 27, it does not appear. In the first of these, the imperfect Cokes Tale is followed by a blank space, and the next written page begins with The Prologue of the Man of Lawe. In the second, the Cokes Tale has, at the point where it breaks off, the significant note—'Of this Cokes tale maked Chaucer na moore,' and the rest of the page is blank ; the next page begins with The Prologue of the Wyf of Bathe. In the Cambridge MS. nearly all of leaf 193 is cut out, and leaf 194 begins with the tenth line of the Man of Lawes Prologue, which must have followed the imperfect Cokes Tale immediately. To these may be added the Cambridge MS. marked Dd. 4. 24, which also ignores the Tale of Gamelyn. On the other hand, it is found in the following ten MSS. at least, viz. the Harleian MSS. nos. 7334 and 1758; the Royal MSS. 18 C. ii and 17 D. xv; MS. Sloane 1685; MS. Lansdowne 851; the Petworth MS.; the MS. in Corpus Christi College, Oxford; and the Cambridge MSS. marked Ii. 3. 26 and Mm. 2. 5. It always appears in the same place, i.e. in the gap left in Chaucer's work by his omission to finish the composition (or, more probably, the revision) of the Cook's Tale. In the well-written Harl. MS. 7334, which affords much the best copy, the scribe, after writing out the 58 lines of the Cokes Tale, is careful to leave the rest of the page blank; and repeats this precaution at the end of Gamelyn. There is, in fact, no connection between this Tale and any work of Chaucer, and no reason for connecting it with the Cook's Tale in particular, beyond the mere accident that the gap here found in Chaucer's work gave an opportunity for introducing it. It is quite clear that some scribes preserved it because they thought it worth preserving, and that it must have been found amongst Chaucer's MSS. in some connection with his Canterbury Tales. We can hardly doubt that he had obtained a copy with the view of making good use of it, and the various copies now extant all agree so closely that they must have been due to a single original. As I have already said once before[1], 'some have supposed, with great reason, that this Tale occurs amongst the rest because it is one which Chaucer intended to recast, although, as a fact, he did not live to re-write a single line of it. This is the more likely because the Tale is a capital one in itself, well worthy of having been re-written even by so great a poet. .... But I cannot but protest against the stupidity of the botcher whose hand wrote above it " The Cokes Tale of Gamelyn[2]."

---

[1] Introduction to The Prioresses Tale, ed. Skeat, p. xv.

[2] Sure enough, in MS. Harl. 7334, this title of ' The Cokes Tale of Gamelyn ' is merely scribbled, as a head-line to the pages, in a much later hand than that of the original scribe.

That was done because it happened to be found *next after* the Cook's Tale, which, instead of being about Gamelyn, is about Perkin the reveller, an idle apprentice.' My remarks continue with the words—'The fitness of things ought to shew at once that this Tale of Gamelyn, a tale of the woods, in the true Robin-Hood style, could only have been placed in the mouth of him "who bare a mighty bow," and who knew all the usage of woodcraft; in one word, of the Yeoman. And we hence obtain the additional hint, that the Yeoman's Tale was to have followed the Cook's Tale, a tale of fresh country-life succeeding one of the close back-streets of the city. No better place can be found for it.' I was much interested in finding, not long ago, that Urry, who first printed the Tale of Gamelyn in 1721, has already said the same thing. At p. 36 of his edition of the Canterbury Tales, he remarks : 'In all the MSS. it is called the Cooke's Tale [1], and therefore I call it so in like manner : But had I found it without an Inscription [2] and had been left to my Fancy to have bestow'd it on which of the Pilgrims I had pleas'd, I should certainly have adjudged it to the Squire's Yeoman : who tho as minutely describ'd by Chaucer, and characteriz'd in the third Place, yet I find no Tale of his in any of the MSS. And because I think there is not any one that would fit him so well as this, I have ventur'd *to place his Picture before this Tale,* tho' I leave the Cook in possession of the *Title.'*

§ 8. It remains to be added that the weight of evidence, even in the MSS. themselves, is actually *against* assigning this Tale to the Cook. I have already said that, in MS. Harl. 7334, such assignment is not in the handwriting of the original scribe. In the Corpus MS., there is no remark except ' Incipit Fabula.' The Royal, Sloane, and Petworth MSS. all call it 'The Tale of ȝong Gamelyn,' and introduce it abruptly with two spurious and halting lines, as follows :—

> ' But here-of I will passe as now
> And of ȝong Gamelyne I wil telle ȝow.'

[1] This is not the fact; *five* of the six MSS. printed by Mr. Furnivall do not mention the Cook at the commencement of the tale, and the final 'rubrics' are of no authority.

[2] This he might easily have done; see the note above.

The Lansdowne MS. introduces it with the following miserable doggerel :—

> 'Fye þer-one, it is so foule, I will nowe tell no forþere,
> For schame of þe harlotrie þat seweþ after;
> A velany it were þare-of more to spell,
> But of a knyhte & his sonnes My tale I wil forþe tell.'

It is true that, at the *end* of Gamelyn, we find, in *four* of the six MSS. printed by Mr. Furnivall, such rubrics as 'Here endith the Cokis tale,' 'Here endeþ the tale of the Coke' (*twice*), and 'Explicit fabula Coci ;' but these remarks are of no value, because the rubricator and the scribe were usually different people, and we constantly find, in MSS. of this period, that the rubricator inserts a wrong capital letter even where the scribe has actually written a very small letter in the corner of the blank space for his information. Here, in like manner, the writers of the rubrics have not observed that the scribes gave them no authority for writing what they did. It is a case of mere carelessness. Similarly, in the Cambridge MS. Mm. 2. 5, the story is simply headed 'The Tale of ӡonge Gamelyn,' but the rubricator who inserted the head-lines has continued the title 'The Cokes Tale,' without any authority, throughout the tale of Gamelyn as well. Hence, when we actually come to such a note as that which precedes Gamelyn in MS. Royal 17 D. xv, viz. 'Her endeth o tale of the Cooke and her folowyth a-nother tale of the same cooke,' we are quite sure that it is a mere blunder, signifying nothing. All the evidence that is worth having certainly informs us that the full correct title is 'The Tale of Yong Gamelyn,' and nothing else. The word 'Yong' may, however, be omitted, and it is now usual to do so.

§ 9. The occurrence of the Tale in such an early MS. as MS. Harl. 7334 is at once a good proof of its antiquity ; whilst at the same time Chaucer must have come by a copy some years before his death (A. D. 1400). When we compare the language with that of Robert of Brunne, who died in 1340, there is no apparent reason why 'Gamelyn' should not have been written at least as early as 1350. Certainly, Robert of Brunne did not himself write Gamelyn, for he would never have penned ll. 491, 492 of the story ; but we shall do well to consider the great influence of this writer, so ably dwelt upon by Mr. Kington Oliphant, who calls him ' The Patriarch of the New English.' (See Old and Middle English, by T. L. Kington Oliphant, 1878, p. 448.) The peculiar metre points to a similar conclusion ; it is rough and irregular, but it is just the same as that which we find in Robert of Gloucester's Chronicle, written in 1298, in the so-called Lives of the Saints sometimes attributed to the same author[1] and written about the same time, and in the *earlier*[2] part of the translation of Langtoft's Chronicle by Robert of Brunne, made between 1327 and 1338. When, in course of time, this metre became perfectly regular, it produced the ' common metre' of our psalm-books and, it may be added, of our ballads. The 'Alexandrine' line of Drayton's Polyolbion is a mere variety of the same, due to the employment of only three accents instead of four in the former half of the line. It is a considerable defect of the metre of Gamelyn that the number of accents in the line is variable. This metre was less in favour towards the end of the fourteenth century, being to some extent superseded, first by the line of four accents as employed by Chaucer in his House of Fame, and by Barbour in his Bruce, and secondly by the line of five accents as employed by Chaucer in his seven-line stanzas, and still later in his couplets. On the whole, I think we may roughly date the Tale of Gamelyn near the middle of the fourteenth century.

§ 10. The connection between the Tale of Gamelyn and Shakespeare's As You Like It, is easily explained. It so happens that none of the black-letter editions of Chaucer contain the Tale, which was, in fact, never printed till 1721, but MSS. of Chaucer circulated amongst readers, and in this way Thomas Lodge became acquainted with it[3], and founded upon it the former part

[1] At any rate he seems to have written The Life of Thomas Beket, a considerable portion of which reappears in his Chronicle.

[2] The later portion introduces additional rimes, in the *middle* of the lines, and is altogether more regular.

[3] He certainly made use of a MS. which gave the name of the old Knight as Sir John of Burdeux (Bourdeaux). I have not as yet met with this in any other than the Cambridge MS. Ii. 3. 26, which has the spelling *burdeuxs*. Mr. Wright says vaguely that ' some MSS. have this reading'; but I suspect this is because he partly collated this very MS. Shakespeare merely follows Lodge.

of a certain novel entitled Euphues' Golden Legacy. Whence he obtained the latter part of the same work does not appear, but it is not improbable that he had it from some Italian novel; for I should hardly be inclined to suppose that it was, after all, of his own invention. It is well known that Shakespeare's play is almost entirely founded on Lodge's novel; and the reader is particularly referred to the copious extracts from Lodge which are given by Mr. Aldis Wright in the Introduction to his edition of As You Like It. As my present object is to shew to what extent Lodge (and indirectly Shakespeare) was indebted to the old tale, I here subjoin such an analysis of Lodge's work as may suffice to indicate the chief points of resemblance.

§ 11. The following is, accordingly, a short sketch of the story as it appears in the novel by Thomas Lodge, entitled 'Euphues go!den Legacie, found after his death in his Cell at Silexedra, bequeathed to Philavtus Sonnes, nvrsed vp with their Father in England'; London, 1592[1].

Sir John of Bourdeaux, Knight of Malta, had three sons, Saladine, Fernandine, and Rosader. On his death-bed, he leaves to the eldest 'foureteen ploughlands, with all my Mannor-houses and richest plate'; to the second, twelve plough-lands; and to the youngest sixteen ploughlands, as well as 'my Horse, my Armour, and my Launce.' Saladine is envious of Rosader, and keeps him in a servile condition, with but little education. In course of a few years, Rosader, 'perceiving his beard to bud[2], for choler began to blush, and swore to himselfe he would be no more subject to such slaverie. As he was thus ruminating of his melancholie passions, in came Saladyne with his men ... Sirha, (quoth he) ... what, is my dinner readie[3]?' Rosader replies, 'Doest thou aske mee, Saladyne, for thy Cates? aske some of thy Churles who are fit for suche an office[4].' Saladine says to his men, 'You, sirs, lay holde on him and binde him, and then I wil give him a cooling carde for his choller[5]. This made Rosader halfe mad, that stepping to a great rake[6]

---

[1] I follow the.convenient reprint (which preserves the old spelling) in Shakespeare's Library, ed. W. C. Hazlitt, vol. ii.

[2] Gamelyn, l. 82.   [3] L. 90.   [4] L. 92.

[5] Ll. 118, 540.   [6] L. 122.

that stood in the garden, hee laide such loade uppon his brothers men that hee hurt some of them, and made the rest of them run away. Saladyne, seeing Rosader so resolute ... thought his heeles his best safetie, and tooke him to a loaft[1] adjoyning to the garden, whether Rosader pursued him hotlie[2].' Saladine deprecates his anger, and adds: 'say wherein thou art discontent and thou shalt bee satisfied[3].' Accordingly, they are reconciled, and 'went into the house arme in arme togither[4].'

This reconciliation, feigned on the part of Saladine, continued till Torismond, king of France, appointed 'a day of Wrastling[5] and of Tournament to busie his Commons heades,' and to turn their thoughts from their former king Gerismond, whom he had driven into banishment. A Norman champion is the challenger; and Saladine bribes him to kill Rosader if he can get the opportunity. Having done this, he persuades Rosader to go to the tournament, taking with him his father's lance, sword, and horse[6]. The twelve peers of France are present at the tournament, together with Alinda, the king's daughter, and Rosalind, daughter of Gerismond. After the tournament comes the wrestling, when the Norman champion violently overthrows and kills the two sons of a franklin of the country[7]. Rosader comforts the franklin, and offers to try and avenge their deaths; the franklin thanks him 'with promise to pray for his happy successe[8].' The champion recognises Rosader, and strains every nerve to subdue him; but is himself violently overthrown and slain[9], which 'highly contented' the franklin[10]. Rosader's name and birth are made known[11], and Rosalind falls in love with him. Rosader also falls in love with Rosalind, and sends her a sonnet.

Saladine is expecting to hear of Rosader's death, when 'he cast up his eye, and sawe where Rosader returned with the garland on his head, as having won the prize, accompanied with a crue of boon companions: greeved at this, he stepped in and shut the gate[12].' Rosader 'ran his foot against the doore,

[1] L. 127. [2] L. 133. [3] L. 154. [4] L. 166.
[5] L. 171. [6] L. 180. [7] L. 201. [8] L. 213.
[9] L. 245. [10] L. 252. [11] L. 226. [12] L. 286.

and brake it open[1]: drawing his sword, and entring boldly into the Hall, where he found none (for all were fled) but one Adam Spencer *an English man*, who had beene an old and trustie servant to Sir John of Bourdeaux[2],' and who took Rosader's part. Rosader invites all the company to a feast, saying, 'I te! you Cavaliers, my Brother hath in his house five tunne of wine[3], and as long as that lasteth, I beshrew him that spares his lyquor[4].' After a great frolic, the guests depart[5]. Adam brings about a reconciliation between the two brethren, feigned (as before) on the part of Saladine.

The story next tells of Rosalind, and presents us with a long soliloquy, in which she laments her father's captivity, and admits to herself that Rosader is 'both beautiful and vertuous.' Here enter King Torismond and his daughter Alinda. Torismond, distrusting Rosalind, banishes her from the court; Alinda pleads for her, but without success, and is herself banished for taking her part.

Alinda and Rosalind depart, the former taking the name of Aliena, and the latter that of Ganimede, in the character of Aliena's page. In their travels, they reach the forest of Arden, whither the banished king Gerismond had also repaired. There they find two shepherds, Montanus and Coridon[6], the former of whom is in love with Phoebe. Aliena buys Coridon's farm, that she and Ganimede may dwell in peace.

Meanwhile Saladine, always on the watch to get the better of Rosader, went one morning to his chamber, 'which being open, hee entred with his crue, and surprised his brother when he was a sleepe, and bound him in fetters, and in the midst of his hall chained him to a post[7].' He leaves him two or three days without food[8]. Adam Spencer takes pity upon Rosader, brings him food secretly, and sets him at liberty[9]. Rosader proposes to attack Saladine at once[10]. But Adam reminds him that the next day is to be a great feast-day, and persuades Rosader to resume his place in the fetters, promising to leave them unlocked, and to have ready 'a couple of good pollaxes, one for you

---

[1] L. 298.   [2] Cf. l. 400.   [3] L. 316.   [4] L. 318.   [5] L. 338.
[6] Shakespeare's Silvius and Corin.   [7] L. 387.   [8] L. 396.
[9] Ll. 425, 417.   [10] L. 430.

and another for mee[1],' adding—'when I give you a wincke[2], shake off your chaines, and let us plaie the men.' This plan is adopted ; and Saladine shews the guests Rosader in chains, alleging that he is mad[3]. Rosader pleads for their pity, but not meeting with success, waits for the signal. This being given, he drops his fetters, and he and Adam seize the pole-axes, and drive all out of the house[4]. Rosader and his friends feast and make merry[5]. Saladine escapes, and applies to the sheriff for help, who takes with him 'five and twentie tall men[6],' and makes for the house. Adam and Rosader determine to make resistance[7]; and, sallying out, break through all opponents, and make good their retreat to the forest of Arden[8]. They suffer from hunger, and are ready to despair, but encourage one another. Rosader says he will go and search the forest, in hope of obtaining assistance ; and finds the banished king Gerismond, who 'with a lustie crue of Outlawes lived in that Forrest,' and was then making a feast to 'his bolde yeomen[9].' Rosader boldly addresses the company, with a threatening aspect. Gerismond has pity on him, and Rosader goes to fetch Adam, whom he finds in a fainting state ; whereupon he 'got him up on his backe, and brought him to the place.' Gerismond hears all Rosader's story[10], and reveals his own name ; finally, he makes Rosader 'one of his forresters[11].' Gerismond is sad at hearing the news of the banishment of Alinda and Rosalind.

Torismond hears of Rosader's flight, and learns that Saladine is now sole heir (as he supposes) to Sir John of Bourdeaux. He determines to quarrel with Saladine, and seize all his property. He sends for Saladine, accuses him, and casts him into prison. Next follows Saladine's soliloquy in prison. The king sends for him, reproves him, and banishes him. Saladine resolves to find out Rosader, and be reconciled to him.

Rosader recalls his love for Rosalind, writes sonnets, and carves his mistress' name upon the trees in the forest. He is

---

[1] L. 445. [2] L. 453. [3] Ll. 465, 385. [4] L. 510.
[5] L. 542. [6] L. 553. [7] L. 587. [8] L. 605.
[9] L. 629. [10] L. 682.
[11] L. 685. From this point to the end the resemblance to the tale of Gamelyn almost ceases.

found by Aliena and Ganimede, who eagerly enquire who is meant by 'Rosalind.' After a while, Rosader reads them three sonnets in Rosalind's praise. Ganimede instructs Rosader how to woo Rosalind, and offers to personate her for the purpose.

Meanwhile Saladine reaches the forest, where he falls asleep, and is espied by a lion, who waits for him to awake. Rosader, coming by that way, slays the lion. Saladine, without recognising Rosader, tells who he is, and expresses deep contrition. Rosader reveals himself, and they are truly reconciled. Rosader presents Saladine to Gerismond, and also conducts him to Adam Spencer. Owing to these events, Rosader sees nothing of Ganimede for three days, when they again meet and discourse.

Meanwhile certain rascals, who prowled about in the forest, determine to seize Aliena and present her to the king, in hope of some reward. Rosader comes to the rescue of Aliena and Ganimede, but is wounded and nearly overpowered; at this instant Saladine also arrives, and the robbers are put to flight. Ganimede dresses Rosader's wounds, whilst Aliena and Saladine discourse tenderly. Aliena and Ganimede, left to themselves, condole with each other on their fortunes. Coridon appears, and brings them to a thicket where they may see Montanus wooing Phoebe, who rejects him scornfully. Ganimede approaches her, and reproves her; but with the strange result that Phoebe is enamoured of Ganimede.

Saladine finds Aliena and Ganimede, and says that his brother's wounds are 'dangerous, but not mortall.' Saladine wooes Aliena, and is accepted.

Phoebe falls ill for love of Ganimede. Montanus, hearing of it, leads Ganimede to Phoebe's house. Phoebe confesses her love, whereupon Ganimede says—'I wil never marry my-selfe to woman but unto thy-selfe.' After this, Ganimede, meeting Rosader, who is now nearly recovered, tells him that he shall see his Rosalind shortly. The marriage-day of Saladine and Aliena is fixed upon, Gerismond and his foresters being invited to the marriage; Montanus and Phoebe are also present. Gerismond hears the story of Montanus' passion, his rejection by Phoebe, and the love of Phoebe for Ganimede. Ganimede is presented to the king, who is at once reminded of his daughter

Rosalind, and sighs. Rosader sighs as deeply, saying that he loves none but Rosalind. Ganimede obtains from Phoebe a promise to marry Montanus, if she can by any means be cured of her present passion. Thereupon Ganimede retires, and reappears in woman's attire, falling at her father's feet. At once two more weddings are agreed upon, that of Rosader with Rosalind, and that of Montanus with Phoebe. Aliena then reveals herself as Alinda, daughter of Torismond.

Whilst the triple wedding-feast is proceeding, Fernandine (the second brother[1]) suddenly arives from Paris, with the startling news that the twelve peers of France are up in arms to dethrone Torismond, and that a battle is imminent, close at hand. Gerismond and the three brothers hurry to the battle-field, where the appearance of Gerismond in person decides the strife, Torismond being slain in the battle. The king is restored to his throne[2], and creates Rosader heir-apparent to the king-dom, makes Saladine duke of Nemours, Fernandine his own secretary, Montanus lord of Arden Forest, Adam captain of the king's guard, and Coridon master of Aliena's flocks.

§ 12. The variableness of the metre renders the poem difficult to scan, and in some places raises doubts as to the grammatical force of the final -*e*. But the grammar will be found to resemble that of Chaucer rather closely, though it is in some points less regular, being of a somewhat more Northern character. The reader may consult the Metrical Analysis of the Squire's Tale, given at p. lxvii of my edition of The Prioresses Tale (third edi-tion, 1880), and the remarks at the end of the Introduction to Dr. Morris's edition of Chaucer's Prologue, &c. Each verse is divided into two parts by a metrical pause, denoted in this edition by a raised full stop (·) ; my marking of the metrical pause is to some extent arbitrary, since the MSS. mostly omit it. It occurs, nevertheless, in several instances, and the assistance to the reader is so great that I have not hesitated to insert it throughout. In MS. Harl. 1758, for instance, we find a slanting stroke / in-troduced as a metrical mark after *a-nother*, l. 444 ; *hider*, l. 531 ; *maister*, l. 668 ; *maister*, l. 669 ; *brother*, l. 727 ; and *togider*, l. 899. In the Petworth MS. such marks are fairly abundant ; thus, in

---

[1] Cf. l. 729.　　　　　　[2] Cf. l. 689.

the passage contained in ll. 21–58, consisting of 38 lines, only 13 lines are unmarked; so that there is quite sufficient authority to guide us to the right method of division. In considering the scansion, it will greatly assist us to consider each half-line separately. If, then, we denote an accented syllable by *A*, and an unaccented syllable by *b*, it will be found that, omitting the less regular lines, the commonest types for the first half-line are the following.

(1) AbAbAb; as in l. 12 :—

> Hów his chíldren schóldë.

So also ll. 15, 21, 22, 23, 26, 28, 49, &c.

(2) bAbAbA; as in l. 37 :—

> And fór the lóv' of Gód.

So also ll. 50, 51, 69, 71, 88, 93, 105.

(3) bAbAbA b; as in l. 2 :—

> And yé schull' hér' a tálkyng.

So also ll. 9, 17, 19, 27, 29, 32, 42, 61, 64.

The above are half lines of *three* accents; but *four* accents occur also, chiefly in the following types.

(4) AbAbAbA; as in l. 120 :—

> Gámelýn was wár anón.

So also ll. 123, 135, 139, 252, 280, 282, 306. Also ll. 199, 207, where *Good-ë* marks the vocative case.

(5) AbAbAbAb; as in l. 34 :—

> Bót' of bálë gód may séndë.

So l. 118, 336.

(6) bAbAbAbA; as in l. 6 :—

> The éldest wás a móchë schréw'.

So also ll. 55 (*neyhëbours* being a trisyllable), 62, 80, 94, 96, 99, 100, 107, 109, 125, 136, 153, &c.

(7) bAbAbAbAb; as in ll. 31, 58 :—

> And séydë, síre, for góddes lóvë.
> That wás my fádres héritágë.

Most of the further variations are caused by the slurring of a slight syllable which is practically superfluous; or, on the other hand, by the omission of an unaccented syllable. The former of these processes is simple and common. Thus, in l. 18, we have :—

To hélpe dél*en his* lóndes,

where the two syllables italicised are run together, and the line is practically of type no. 3.

It is the other process, the omission of a syllable, which jars so disagreeably upon the modern ear. Thus, e. g., in l. 23, we have the half-line :—

Ón his déth-bédde.

And again, in l. 41, the half-line :—

Tho lété théy the kníght lýen.

And, in l. 68, the half-line :—

And déydë whán týmë cóm.

Yet the fact is, that this unpleasant effect is by no means uncommon in our nursery rimes, where, through old association, it is hardly noticed as a defect. In the rime of ' Sing a song of six-pence,' which has exactly the lilt of many lines in Gamelyn, the last line usually runs—And snápp'd óff her nóse. We cannot doubt that the old poem was considered, in its time, sufficiently musical.

§ 13. The latter half-line is usually shorter, and less varied. A large number of them will be found to conform to the types above containing three accents, viz. nos. 1, 2, and 3. Like no. 1 are the latter halves of ll. 3, 9 (*lyuede* being trisyllabic), 16, 17, 20, 41, 50, 58, 64, 73, 74, &c. Like no 2 are the latter halves of ll. 1, 7, 8, 26, 32, 34, 35, 36, 44, 45, 87, 88, &c. Like no. 3 are the latter halves of ll. 10, 18, 19, 28, 39, 42, 57, 63, 68, &c. But some half-lines are still shorter, and present a type similar to no. 1 when docked of its last syllable, so as to become AbAbA. Examples are: ón his faíre fél, 76 ; nówther ȝóng ne óld, 79 ; and in ll. 107, 109, 128, 131, 132, 135, 136, &c. When an unaccented syllable is dropped, we even get such half-lines as—sík thér he láy, 11 ; sík thát he láy, 21 ; whán he góod cówdë, 48 ; he láy stóon-stíllë, 67 ; and the like. Whether the number of accents in the latter half-line is ever allowed to be diminished to *two*, may perhaps be doubted. I suspect that, in reciting the lines slowly, a fictitious additional accent was placed upon the *italicised* syllables in such half-lines as :—by sé-ẏnt[1] *Mar*-tẏn, 53 ; wálk-*yng*-ĕ tháre, 89 ; be bé-*ten* anón, 115; and árt *so* yíng, 148 ; a rám *and* a rẏng, 172; to wéndë *ther*-tó, 173.   But this is a slippery matter, which I leave to the reader's discretion.   I will merely say that no one who is not well acquainted with the rules for the scansion of Chaucer has much chance of success in scanning Gamelyn. The best he can do is to pronounce every final -*e* as a distinct syllable (unless it is obviously elided or very much in the way), to treat the terminations -*ed* and -*es* as forming distinct syllables, to lay a heavy stress on every accented syllable, to pronounce the words *very slowly and deliberately*, using the old pronunciation as described in my Introduction to Chaucer's Man of Law's Tale, p. x ; and *then* perhaps he may trust to a well-trained ear. Perhaps the most important of all these hints is that which enjoins slowness and deliberation.   If read rapidly after the modern fashion, there may still seem to be a sufficient metre ; but it will have no sort of resemblance to that with which the author was himself familiar.

§ 14. A few remarks upon the rimes may be useful. We find both single rimes, as ar*ight*, kn*ight*, 1, 2 ; and double rimes, as n*am*-e, g*am*-e, 3, 4.   The number of double rimes is larger than might be supposed, because many of them are due to the occurrence of final -*e*, which a modern reader is so apt to neglect; thus we have again ʒor-e, sor-e, 9, 10, with similar pairs in 15, 16, 19, 20, 23, 24, &c.   More obvious double rimes occur in kn*ight*-es, to-r*ight*-es, 17 ; *oth*-er, br*oth*-er, 39 ; see also 61, 85, 97, 141, 143, &c.   We find *two* riming with *go* and *so*, 45, 431; this was doubtless a perfect rime at that date, the vowel being pronounced as *oa* in *oak* ; so that *two* was *twoa*.   We find *spencer* with an additional accent on the latter syllable, and riming with *yeer* and *dyner*, 403, 645.   We find the curious spelling *hire* for *here*, in order to force a rime with *sire*, 221; this seems to intimate that the word *here* was, even at this early date, occasionally pronounced as it is at the present day[2]. We find *noon* riming with *Johan*, 365 ; the latter word was pro-

---

[1] Curiously enough, *se-int* seems to have been occasionally dissyllabic, as in Chaucer's Prologue, l. 697.

[2] We find *desire* rimed with *nere* in the Romaunt of the Rose, l, 1785.

nounced like the modern *Joan*. I may remark that the rime *hye*, *ye*, 333, is a double one; both words are dissyllabic, *hy-ë*, *y-ë*, the *y* being pronounced as *i* in *antique*. Some of the rimes are imperfect; thus *wyt*, *bet*, 111, is incorrect. *Now*, *now*, 93, is a mere repetition, and not a true rime at all. *Gat-e*, *skap-e*, 575, form a mere assonance; i.e. they are mere vowel-rimes, the identity of consonants being neglected. We find just the very same assonance in the Romaunt of the Rose, where *shape* rimes with *make*, 2260; *escape* with *make*, 2753; and *take* with *scape*, 3165. It will be observed that the voiceless stopped consonants *t*, *p*, and *k* were considered as approaching to identity. The only thoroughly bad rime is that of *chanoun* with *nom*, 781, which is made still worse by its false grammar. *Nom* is not the true form of the infinitive, but should have been *nim*; the author actually employs the true past tense singular *nam*, 733, and the true past participle *nom-e*, 584, 683, 796; but again errs in employing *nam* (instead of *namen*, *name*, *nomen*, or *nome*) in l. 216; where the *plural* form is wanted. These false rimes are quite enough to shew that Chaucer was not the author.

§ 15. As to the grammatical forms, a few words may suffice; for I have already said that they are much the same as in Chaucer, but a little less particular; the greater strictness which should consist with an earlier date being more than counterbalanced by the tendency to simplicity of a slightly more Northern dialect. The chief suffixes are the following.

The suffix *-es* is common in the plural of substantives, as *knight-es*, 17, *lond-es*, 18, &c.; in the genitive case singular, as *godd-es*, 24; *fadr-es*, 58; *Gamelyn-es*, 64; and in adverbs, as *on-es*, 234.

The suffix *-ed* occurs in past participles, as *dress-ed*, 15. But it is also common as a shortened form of *-ed-e*, the true ending of the past tense of many weak verbs; as *lou-ed* (for *lou-ed-e* or *lou-ed-en*, plural), 7; *deseru-ed* (for *deseru-ed-e*), 8. The full form, as *lyu-ed-e*, 9, is less common than in Chaucer.

The suffix *-en* is not very common, except as the sign of the infinitive, as in *lyu-en*, 27; or as the sign of the past tense plural, as *went-en*, 42; *dalt-en*, 45; *let-en*, 46. It is also a sign of the past participle of strong verbs, as *i-broken*, 85; *get-en*, 108; *bet-en*, 115; it is shortened to *n* in *bor-n* (for *bor-en*, 108):

y-doo-n, 54. In all three cases the final *-en* is frequently reduced to final *-e* [1].

The suffix *-eth* occurs in the third person singular of the indicative mood, as *draw-eth*, 28 ; but it also denotes the imperative plural, as *dress-eth*, 36 ; *forget-ith = forget-eth*, 38 ; *tak-eth*, 39 ; and is shortened to *-th* in *go-th*, 36.

I shall conclude these remarks upon the grammar by specifying some of the principal uses of the final *-e*, numbering them in the same way as in my remarks upon the Metre of the Squire's Tale (see Introd. to The Prioresses Tale, &c., p. lxx).

1. *Nouns of A.S. origin and of dissyllabic form.* Wille, 28, A.S. *willa* ; mete, 90, A.S. *mete* ; schame, 99, A.S. *sceamu* ; name, 100, A.S. *nama* ; dore, 127, A.S. *duru* ; steede, 187, A.S. *stéda* ; fare, 199, A.S. *faru* ; moone, 235, A.S. *móna* ; eye, 253, A.S. *ege*, i. e. terror ; pleye, 254, A.S. *plega* ; erthe, 300, A.S. *eorče* ; teene, 303, A.S. *téona* ; y-ë, 334, A.S. *éage* ; herte, 335, A.S. *heorte* ; &c. There are many more, the discovery of which will afford good exercise in etymology [2].

2. *Nouns of French origin.* These are not numerous, owing to the small percentage of words of French origin, very different from that which we find in Chaucer. Thus in ll. 43–52 we have ten consecutive lines without a word of French. Examples are: heritage, 58, O.F. *heritagë* ; queste, 64, O.F. *questë* ; paire, 188, O.F. *peirë, pairë* ; place, 210, 213, O.F. *placë* ; feste, 327, O.F. *festë* ; gyle, 369, O.F. *guilë* ; &c.

3. *Dative Cases.* These occur chiefly after the prepositions *at, by, for, in, of, on, to, vp-on, vn-to.* Examples: bedde, 24, A.S. *bedde*, dat. of *bed* ; halle, 77, A.S. *healle*, dat. of *heal* ; ȝerde, 81, A.S. *gearde*, dat. of *geard* ; foote, 109, A.S. *fóte* (as well as *fét*), dat. of *fót* ; hepe, 124, A.S. *héape*, dat. of *héap* ; lyue, 157, A.S. *lífe*, dat. of *líf* ; ore, 159, A.S. *áre*, dat. of *ár*, i. e. grace, favour ; &c.

---

[1] As a sign of a plural substantive we have only the examples *brether-en*, 48 ; *hos-en*, 269. Compare *both-en*, 625 ; *schoo-n*, 269. Examples of adverbs are *sith-en*, 900 ; *bysid-en*, 171. A preposition is *without-en*, 313. The *-en* in *gam-en*, 290, is an essential part of the word.

[2] Owing to the confusion of suffixes in the Middle-English period, we find words with final *-e* that are hardly entitled to them. Hence *berde* for *berd*, 82 ; &c.

4. *Genitive Cases.* These are rare; but we find halle, 461, 496, A.S. *healle*, gen. of *heal.* So also Soneday, 434, A.S. *sunnan dæg*, day of the sun, is an older form than Sonday, 459; the form here varies with the metre.

5. *Adjectives: Definite form.* The definite form is used when the adjective is preceded by *the, this, that,* or a possessive pronoun. Examples: his righte, 3; The goode, 9; that ilke, 30; my 30nge, 38; that grete, 117; the 30nge, 190; The false, 192; the grete, 285; the faire, 310; &c.

6. *Adjectives: Plural forms.* Ex.: alle stille, 54; bothe, 74; goode, 496, 592. So also the numerals fyue, 57, 59; fiftene, sixtene, 358; twelue, 652.

7. *Adjectives: Vocative Case.* Ex.: Goode, 199, 207. Examples are rare.

8. *Adjectives: other inflexions.* Some adjectives, by confusion with the definite form, take a final -*e*. Hence: a false, 168. In most cases, however, the final -*e* can be accounted for etymologically. Thus moche, 6, 275, is short for *mochel* or *muchel*, A.S. *mycel*; 3are, 90, is A.S. *gearu*; worse, 107, is A.S. *wyrsa*.

9. *Verbs: Infinitive Mood.* The final -*e* is short for -*en*, A.S. -*an.* Ex.: speke, 20; sende, 34; haue, 44; wraththe, 80; come, 120; lepe, 123; bygynne, 132; ryde, 312.

10. *Verbs: Gerundial Infinitive.* Known by the use of *to* preceding it; A.S. -*anne.* Ex.: To helpe, 18; t'abyde, 24; to bete, 118; for to ryde, 177.

11. *Strong Verbs: Past Participles.* The right suffix is -*en*, as to-broken, 97; but the final -*n* is often dropped, the -*e* being preserved. Ex.: i-nome, 119; flowe, 133; holde, 248; i-steke, 329; y-bounde, 397.

12. *Weak Verbs: Past tense in* -de or -te. Ex.: (*a*) cowde, 4; lyuede (with full suffix -*ed-e*), 9; scholde, 12; hadde, 13, 307; deyde, 68; dede, 75; wolde, 80; sayde, 297. Some common words can drop the final -*e* at times, especially before a vowel; hence: loked (for lokede), 125. Ex.: (*b*) dalte, 65; aboughte, 76; wente, 88; wiste, 167, 369; kiste, 168; caste, 237[1].

---

[1] These verbs, with the past tenses in -*de* or -*te*, all *invariably* lose the final -*e* in the past participle, which in A.S. ends in -*od* or -*ed*. Just so, in German, if the past tense is *brachte*, with final -*e*, the pp is *gebracht*, without it. Hence the pp. i-had, 357; wist, 393. It seems a

13. *Verbs: Subjunctive Mood.* Ex.: stonde, i. e. may stand, 64; graunte, i. e. may grant, 154. Not common.

14. *Verbs: various other inflexions.* Ex.: (*a*) 1 p. pr. indicative; warne, 26; beseke (probably pronounced bysek', for euphony), 35; byquethe, 62; telle, 371; byseche, 399. (*b*) 2 p. imper. sing. of weak verbs; aske, 153, A.S. *ásca*, imper. s. of *áscian* or *ácsian*; loke, 154, A.S. *lóca*, imper. s. of *lócian*; so also the French verb graunte, 149, by analogy.

Besides these examples, we find (*c*) the remarkable use of -*e* in the 2nd pers. sing. of the pt. t. of strong verbs, as in Anglo-Saxon; where modern English has substituted -*est*. Ex.: spake, 94; come, i. e. camest, 222; knewe, 224; threwe, 372. Moreover, the strong verbs, which *never* (except in the second person) take a final -*e* in the past tense *singular*, do so in the plural; hence: they drowe, 130, pl. of drow; gonne, 236, pl. of gan, 130.

15. *Adverbs.* Ex.: sone, 6, 132; Selde, 40; stille, 50, 102; wrothe, 73; algate, 115; swithe sore, 152; byside, 178, 183; wyde, 311; stronge, 397; longe, 398; &c. By analogy we even find there (riming with were), 251; here, 282; though the A.S. forms are *đær, hér*. These are not solitary examples; Chaucer likewise has *there* riming with *were*, in the Pardoneres Tale, Group C, l. 689; whilst *here* is distinctly dissyllabic in the Ormulum, l. 3264.

To the above examples of adverbs we may add the *preposition* withoute, 26, 259, short for *withouten*.

We must also be careful to observe that -*e*- sometimes forms a distinct syllable in the middle of a word. Ex.: wyd-e-wher, 13; smert-e-ly, 187, 243, 247; auaunc-e-ment, 418; Iugg-e-ment, 750; wrast-e-lyng, 194.

§ 16. The text here printed is based upon the Harleian MS. 7334 in the British Museum, which is much the best and oldest of the MSS. containing the Tale. By careful collation with other MSS., I have improved the text in several places, but it will be found that the alterations are almost all of a very slight character, and in many cases concern the question of adding a final -*e*. In no case have I made the *slightest* deviation from

simple matter; yet many students are wholly incapable of parsing *wiste* and *wist*, or of making any distinction between them.

the above MS. without noting the fact in the footnotes, and giving the names of the MSS. which support the alteration, or at any rate saying what reading I propose. Thus in l. 3, the word *right* ought grammatically to be *righte*, but I cannot in this instance give my authority, because all the MSS. (except the best) unluckily and wrongly omit the word altogether. The student who desires further information may consult the Sixtext edition of Chaucer's Canterbury Tales, printed for the Chaucer Society by Mr. Furnivall. There the following MSS. are printed *in extenso*, viz. the Royal MS. 18 C. ii (which I denote by Rl.), also in the British Museum; the Harleian MS. no. 1758, in the same library[1]; the Sloane MS. no. 1685, in the same library (denoted by Sl.)[2]; the MS. in Corpus Christi College, Oxford (denoted by Cp.); the Petworth MS. (Pt.), belonging to Lord Leconfield; and the Lansdowne MS. no. 851, in the British Museum (Ln.). I have also consulted, occasionally, two MSS. in the Cambridge University Library, marked respectively Ii. 3. 26 and Mm. 2. 5. It may be noted that many of the MSS. have lost various lines, owing to the carelessness of the scribes. Thus Rl. omits ll. 281, 282, 283, 375, 376, 377, 731, 813, 814. Harl. 1758 omits 281, 282, 375, 376, 813, 814. Sl. omits 281, 282, 375, 376, 377, 441, 442, 496, 813, 814; and MS. Royal 17 D. xv. omits 856, 857. Cp., which is the second best copy, omits l. 264. Pt. omits 281, 282, 375, 376, 813, 814. Ln. omits 263, 264, 265, 341, 342, 343, 344, 731, 733, 769, 770. The agreement between the MSS. is remarkably close, and the chief differences are in the spelling. The word *com*, supplied in l. 550 from the two Cambridge MSS., should perhaps be *wente*; the omission of the verb in the other copies is curious, as it leaves both sense and scansion imperfect. In l. 629, Mr. Wright supplied the word *in* before *compas*, but without any better authority (as far as I can see) than Urry's edition. So also in l. 444, he inserted *thing* after *another*, on the same authority. The true reading of almost every line can be sufficiently ascertained.

[1] This copy is imperfect, having lost ll. 1–13; these 13 lines are supplied by Mr. Furnivall from the Royal MS. marked 17 D. xv.

[2] This copy is imperfect at the end, after l. 826; the remainder is supplied from the same Royal MS., viz. 17 D. xv.

§ 17. The previous editions of the Tale may be briefly described. I have already said that it was first printed by Urry in 1721, in his edition of Chaucer. His spellings of the words are so fantastical, and the whole of his work so worthless and absurd, that it is hardly even possible to say what MS. he used. This miserable version was reprinted in Chalmers' English Poets, i. 607, in 1810. Tyrwhitt omitted it in his edition of the Canterbury Tales, quite rightly, on the ground that Chaucer had no hand in it. Mr. Wright first printed it from the best MS., viz. Harl. 7334, in the Percy Society's edition of the Canterbury Tales, distinguishing it from the genuine Tales by the use of smaller type. He followed the MS. very closely, but somewhat carelessly omitted three lines, viz. ll. 563, 601, 602; which throws out the correct numbering of the lines. Wright's text was reprinted in Bell's edition of Chaucer, but without comparison with the MS.; consequently, the same three lines are omitted there also. Finally, Dr. Morris again reprinted Wright's text in his edition of Chaucer, but with more care, discovering and supplying the three missing lines, and making a few corrections; whilst Mr. Furnivall, in his Six-text edition, printed six other MSS. (as said above), purposely omitting MS. Harl. 7334, owing to its having already thrice appeared in print. It will hence be understood that the texts as given by Wright, Bell, and Morris are all much the same, and represent the same MS.; Dr. Morris's text being the most correct of the three. In some places Dr. Morris has purposely made slight alterations; it will suffice to add that in lines 166, 212, 405, 426, 528, 773, 785, 857, 877, he has followed Mr. Wright's text rather than the MS., but there is no difference sufficiently important to need further comment.

§ 18. A carefully written critical examination of The Tale of Gamelyn, by F. Lindner, appeared in the Englische Studien, ed. E. Kölbing, vol. ii. pp. 94, 321 (1878). He seems, however, to have committed the singular error of confusing MS. Harl. 1758 with MS. Harl. 7334, not being aware of the existence of *two* copies of our poem in the Harleian collection. This is very unfortunate, because he has consequently omitted to consult the readings of MS. Harl. 7334, which is much the best copy, and would have solved many of his difficulties. Hence he speaks of the text in Bell's Chaucer as being printed from 'the Harleian MS.,' and notices that it *varies considerably* from it [1] ; meaning, as I suppose, that it varies considerably from MS. Harl. 1758.   No doubt it does ; for Bell's text is a mere copy of Wright's text, and the latter represents (very faithfully upon the whole, though with the unlucky omission of three lines) the *other* Harl. MS., No. 7334.   Elsewhere he draws the conclusion that the best copy is to be found in the Corpus MS., because it omits only *one* line ; the fact being that MS. Harl. 7334 is perfect, and omits no line at all.   Yet most of his conclusions are quite correct, and his criticisms just.   It is interesting to find that, even without the assistance of the best MS., he was able to see that all the copies really go back to *one* original ; that the Corpus MS. is 'the best,' i. e. the *next* best to Harl. 7334 ; that the Lansdowne MS. most closely agrees with the Corpus MS.; and that the other MSS. give inferior readings, the Sloane MS. being the worst.   I can only indicate very briefly some of Lindner's results, and must refer the reader to the original article for further information.

He remarks that Gamelyn was first composed for recitation ; observe the frequent repetition of *litheth*, i. e. listen ye, at the beginning of each section of the lay ; see ll. 1, 169, 289, 341, 551, 769 ; cf. l. 615.   For a comparison of Gamelyn with Lodge's novel, he refers us to Delius' edition of Shakespeare, ii. 347 (1872).   At p. 101 he gives us a complete Rime-index to the whole poem, and at p. 107 notices the false rimes on which I have already commented ; also the repetitions of *now*, 93 ; *other*, 445 ; *the*, 363, 399.   The rimes are mostly of the most ordinary character, and the poem is very inartificial ; see, e. g., ll. 135–138, 261–270, 315–318, 529–534, 649–652, 729–732, 811–814 ; &c.   The author constantly repeats himself ; note the repetition of *sore* in ll. 10, 11 ; *for to dele*, 42, 43 ; also ll. 72, 73 ; 85, 86, compared with 97, 98 ; *al that my fader me byquath*, 99, 157, 160, 360 ; 120, 121 ; 149, 150, compared with 151–154 ; 190, 191, &c.   Short expressions or 'tags' occur over and over again ; as, *ther he lay*, 11, 21, 25, 33, 50, 52, 66 ; *Cristes curs mot he haue*, 106, 114, 116, 818 ; *by Cristes ore*, 139, 159, 231, 323 ; *he bigan*

---

[1] ' Eine ausgabe, welche bedeutende abweichungen von dem Harleian MS. aufweist ;' p. 95, note.

to goon, 126, 220, 236, 498 ; *euel mot ʒe thee*, 131, 363, 448, 720 ; cf. 379, 413, 577 ; *whil he was on lyue*, 20, 58, 157, 225, 228. There are frequent examples of alliteration, as *litheth and lesteneth*, 1, 169, &c.; *bote of bale*, 32, 34, 631 ; *stondeth alle stille*, 55 ; *stoon-stille*, 67, &c. ; which the reader may easily find. We also find repetitions of ideas, the latter part of the verse merely reproducing the former ; as in 107, 174, 217, 221, 381, 699, 732. The proportion of French words in ' Gamelyn ' is much less than in Chaucer. A description of the MSS. is given at p. 321 (where MS. Harl. 7334 is not mentioned). At p. 324 is an analysis of some of the looser rimes, according to the various spellings of the MSS. The rime *thare, ʒare*, 89, 793, is certainly Northern. Observe *ʒing, kyng*, 887 [1]. At p. 328 is a full analysis of the grammatical forms and of varieties of spelling. At p. 113, Lindner is inclined to connect the story of Gamelyn with the time of Fulke Fitz Warin, i.e. with the time of King John ; see Ten Brink, Early English Literature, Eng. version, p. 149. At p. 321, he says that the description of Gamelyn's brother's house, with its hall-door (461), outer gate (286), postern-gate (589), bower (405), &c. suits the description of an Anglo-Norman manor-house of the thirteenth century ; see Wright, A History of English Culture, London, 1874. The father of the hero was evidently a Norman knight ; cf. l. 108. See also the note (by Jephson) in Bell's edition, to l. 892 ; 'This is the usual *dénouement* of all the tales of this class, and it may possibly be founded upon fact. For it might be sound policy on the king's part to enlist the services of a bold and popular outlaw, like Gamelyn, in the cause of order, at a time when personal valour and daring were often able to set the law at defiance. An honest but inexperienced and unwarlike magistrate would have been of very little use in a forest in Nottinghamshire [2] in the thirteenth century.' Lindner emphasises the word *thirteenth* (which may easily have been a mistake for fourteenth,

---

[1] On the other hand, we have *tonge, yonge*, 169. I suspect that dialectal variations enabled some of our poets, especially those who only composed for recitation, to be not very particular.

[2] Here the *locality* of the poem is assumed without proof ; however, the statement would apply to other counties.

such mistakes being extremely common), and unhesitatingly attributes our poem to the thirteenth century. Here I do not hesitate to say, that it is certainly not earlier than 1320 (see p. xiii. above, l. 26), as the language plainly shews. That it may *refer* to the thirteenth century is another matter ; but, even so, there is no need to suppose it to refer to a time much earlier than A.D. 1300. The 'Outlaw's Song of Trailbaston,' printed in Wright's Political Songs, p. 231, is worth consulting as shewing the spirit of those times, and we know that this song cannot have been composed before April 6, 1305. If we assign the composition of Gamelyn to about 1340, I do not think we shall be far wrong.

§ 19. INDEX OF FRENCH WORDS IN THE TALE OF GAMELYN. The following is a list of such French words as I have observed in the Tale ; I hope I have included all of them.

Allowe, 578 ; armure, 98 ; aspied, 392, 490 ; assise, 870, 889 ; assoile, 449 (assoiled, 516) ; auauncement, 418 ; auentures, 777 ; auntre, 217, 666 ; auow, 378.

Baillye, 709 ; barre, 852, 860, 867 ; beestes, 359 ; (bi)gyled, 369 ; bokeler, 136 ; bourde, 858.

Cark, 760 ; catour, 321; champioun, 203, 218, 219, 223, 227, 233, 236, 237, 239, 243, 249, 253, 255, 261, 266, 273 ; chanoun, 509, 781 ; charite, 451, 513 ; chaunce, 746 ; chef, 891 ; chere, 319, 534 ; company, 310, 317, 565, 854 ; compas, 629 ; contek, 132 ; continaunce, 262 ; couenant, 414 ; counseil, 42, 456, 683 ; courser, 176 (coursers, 181, 611) ; croune, 523, 671 ; crouned, 660, 694, 695 ; crie, 710, 722, 874 (cryed, 171, 183, 700) ; cuntre, 17.

Delay, 791 ; delyuer, 751 (delyuered, 753) ; delyueraunce, 745 ; deserued, 8 ; dette, 512 ; dismay, 31, 623, 763 ; dol(fully), 475 ; dout, *v.* 517 (doutiden, 78) ; doute, *s.* 630 ; dressen, 18, 848 (dressed, 15 ; dresseth, 36) ; dure, 831 ; dyner, 645.

Endite, 698, 722 (endited, 710) ; enemys, 896 ; enquered, 862.

Faile, 448, 586 (faileth, 446) ; false, 168, 192, 351, 363, 383, 463, 471, 615, 697, 723, 739, 784, 800, 859, 883 (fals, 392 ; falsnes, 164, 884) ; faith, 868 ; fay, 555 ; feire, 270 ; feste, 327, 339, 459 ; folye, 884 ; fool, 222, 274 ; forest, 891 ; frankeleyn, 197, 201, 211, 251, 253, 275 ; frere, 529, 533 ; fyn, *adj.* 681 ; fyn, *s.* 551.

Galys, 277, 764 ; gentil, 663 (gentil-men, 267) ; grace, 630, 725,
815 ; graunte, 149, 154, 156, 744, 751 ; greeue, 313 ; grucche,
319 (grucching, 322, 325) ; gyle, *s.* 369, 562, 580 ; gyled, 70.

Heir, 365, 366, 897 (eyr, 40) ; heritage, 58. Ire, 698.

Iames, 277 (Iame, 665, 764, 797) ; Iohan, 3, 57, 226, 366 ; ioye,
284, 758, 902 ; ioli(ly), 527 ; Iugge(man), 843 ; Iuggement,
750 ; Iustice, 742, 749, 761, 766, 790, 792, 794, 799, 805, 823,
826, 835, 843, 845, 849, 859, 868, 869, 879, 890, 891 (Iustices,
855, 857).

Large, 514 (largely, 324, 520) ; lettres, 19 ; lewte, 657 ; lyoun,
125 ; lyuerey, 514.

Maister (mayster), 256, 637, 639, 656, 658, 660, 668, 669, 677,
683, 686, 688, 694, 776, 834, 876 (maistres, 314) ; mangerye,
345, 434, 464 ; Martyn, 53, 225 ; Maryes, 322, 480 ; messager,
729 ; maynpris, 744 ; mercy, 874 ; messes, 467 ; meyne, 575.

Norture, 4.

Office, 894 ; ordeyne, 798 (ordeyned, 878) ; ordres, 533 ; Ote,
727 (*and* 18 *times more*).

Paire, 188 ; pantrye, 495 ; *par ma foy*, 367 ; parauenture, 642 ;
parde, 743 ; part, *s.* 16 ; parten, 317, 410 ; party, 392 ; passe,
516, 596 ; passioun, 477 ; pay, 514 ; pees, 102, 139, 548, 689,
889 ; pestel, 122, 128, 138, 140, 152 ; peyned, 261 ; place, 195,
203, 210, 213, 216, 263, 267 ; porter, 287, 295, 303, 326, 559,
561, 566, 567, 571, 573, 577, 580 ; post, 387, 437 ; posterne,
589 ; power, 846 ; preuen, 174 (prouen, 242 ; i-proued, 241) ;
prest, 237, 830 ; priour, 487, 492, 509 (priours, 435, 781) ;
prisoun, 442, 478, 481, 726, 741, 796 ; y-prisoned, 737 ;
priue, 425 ; prow, 361 ; prys, 772 ; purchas, 14, 61 ; purs,
321, 885.

Quest, 786, 801, 840, 842, 862, 871, 878 ; queste, 64 ; quitte,
512, 896.

Route, 600 (rowte, 285) ; Rycher, 137, 175, 357, 619.

Seller, 316 (selleer, 351) ; seruantz, 544 ; serue, 468 (serued,
404, 467, 469, 544) ; seynt, 53, 137, 174, 225, 277, 322, 357, 451,
480, 513, 619, 665, 765, 797 ; sire (sir), 3, 221, 696 (*and* 18
times more) ; sisours, 871, 881 ; skape, 576, 825 ; solas, 328 ;
soper, 425 ; spenden, 320 (spende, 324 ; spended, 362) ; spence,
424 ; spense, 320 ; spenser, 398, 399, 493, 501, 618, 620, 646 ;
stoor, 354 ; strif, 549, 758 ; stroye, 354 ; stryue, 158.

Toret, 329 ; tornes, 237, 241, 244 ; trauail, 301 ; traytour, 406 ; trecherie, 346, 463, 883 ; tresoun, 165, 168, 393.

Verrey, 14; vilonye, 721.

Wardeynes, 279 ; wasten, 330 ; wicket, 563 (wyket, 298).

§ 20. I have already spoken of the literary interest of the Tale of Gamelyn, especially in connection with the Robin Hood ballads and As You Like It. It is remarkable as being a story without a heroine ; no female name is even mentioned in it, and it is only in the fifth line from the end that we are told that the hero 'wedded a wife both good and fair.' Hence it is not surprising that Lodge thought it necessary to expand the story, and to provide a Rosalind for his Rosader, to the great gain of our literature. From a purely linguistic point of view, I believe that the Tale is of considerable value, as affording a fair specimen of the East-Midland dialect as spoken more than five hundred years ago. The spelling of every word in the poem deserves careful attention, as possessing a phonetic value far exceeding the conventional system now in use. The Notes explain the more difficult phrases and allusions, and the Glossarial Index includes all the words which can cause any difficulty. For the etymology of such words as are still in use, I beg leave to refer the reader to my Etymological Dictionary of the English Language, either in the larger or in the 'Concise' form. In writing the Notes, I have gladly availed myself of such brief notes as are given by Mr. Wright and by Mr. Jephson (who annotated Bell's Chaucer) ; to which I have added many from other sources.

In conclusion, I have to express my sense of the great help afforded me by Mr. Furnivall's Six-text edition of Chaucer, the readings of which I have implicitly followed. I am also much obliged to Professor Hales and Mr. Oliphant for some hints which have proved helpful in writing this Introduction ; and I must refer all who desire further information about Robin Hood to the remarks by Professor Hales upon the Percy Folio MS., as edited by Mr. Furnivall and himself. The reader may also consult Wright's Essays on the Literature of England in the Middle Ages, and the remarks in vol. v of Professor Child's English and Scotch Ballads, where it is ingeniously suggested that the name *Hood* may be a corruption of 'ood, well-known as a common provincial corruption of the word wood; so that Robin Hood may have meant, at first, no more than Robin of the Wood. In fact, the following remarkable stanza, which seems to point clearly in the same direction, occurs in the ballad of the 'Birth of Robin Hood' in Mr. Allingham's Ballad-book, where it is said to have been 'taken down from recitation without the alteration of a single word.' Earl Richard discovers that his daughter has given birth to a son in the greenwood, whereupon

> He kist him o'er and o'er again,
> 'My grandson I thee claim;
> And Robin Hood *in gude greenwood*,
> 'Tis that shall be your name.'

Peele, the dramatist, in his play of Edward I., speaks expressly of 'Robin of the Wood, *alias* Robin Hood'; see Greene and Peele's Works, ed. Dyce, p. 403, col. 1. 'It is curious,' says Professor Child at p. xxv of his Introduction, 'that Orlando in As You Like It (who represents the outlaw Gamelyn in the Tale of Gamelyn, a tale which clearly belongs to the cycle of Robin Hood) should be the son of Sir Roland *de Bois*. Robin de Bois, says a writer in Notes and Queries, vi. 597, occurs in one of Sue's novels as a well-known mythical character, whose name is employed by French mothers to frighten their children.' I may add that Leigh Hunt, in his Songs of Robin Hood, makes Gamelyn de Vere Robin's uncle, talks of Gamelyn Hall and Gamelyn wood, and introduces Will Scarlet as one of Gamelyn de Vere's serving-men; all of which seems to be rather a strange jumble. I have more sympathy with the pleasing lines by Keats :—

> 'Gone, the merry morris din,
> Gone, the song of Gamelyn;
> Gone, the tough-belted outlaw
> Idling in the "grenè shawe"...
>   So it is; yet let us sing
> Honour to the old bow-string!
> Honour to the bugle-horn!
> Honour to the woods unshorn!
> Honour to the Lincoln green!
> Honour to the archer keen!'

The 'song of Gamelyn' is not yet quite 'gone'; and I shall be glad if this edition helps to revive it.

ADDITIONAL NOTES.

30. The insertion of *ne* seems (to us) required for the sense. Yet Zupitza has shewn that M. E. writers often omit it in such a position. The explanation is a psychological one; i. e. the statement refers to what is *positive*, and thus needs no negative.

43, 45. An apparent contradiction. L. 43 expresses their first intention; l. 45 expresses what they did upon second thoughts.

130. Perhaps insert *hem* after *drowe*, as in Rl. Harl. Sl. Pt. Cf. l. 308.

150. The insertion of *oo* after *Of* is not absolutely necessary; cf. Sir Tristram, 406 (Zupitza).

172. So also in Robert of Brunne, Handlyng Synne, ll. 990-992 :—

> ȝyf þou euer settyst swerde eyþer ryng
> For to gadyr a wrastlyng,
> þe halyday þou holdest noghte.

349, 350. These lines are anticipatory; this raises no difficulty.

351. *Selleer* is certainly an error for *soleer*, i.e. an upper room; see l. 329, and cf. l. 316.

392. *A party*, partly, in some degree; cf. P. Pl. B. xv. 17.

461. *Read*—And euer atte halle dore · as they comen in (Zupitza).

626. The words *him thought* are parenthetical.

780. The word *ferde* (see Glossary) is not the pt. t. of *faren*, but of M. E. *feren*, a derivative of *faren*. M. E. *feren*=A. S. *féran*, derived from *fór*, pt. t. of *faran*.

782. *Nom* (for *nim*) occurs again as an infin. in Shoreham, p. 120, l. 80. The past tense *nam* suggested it; compare *come*, as being the infinitive corresponding to *cam*.

786. Though *quest* here means the jury, the word originally referred to the process of enquiry of trial, and is short for *inquest*, more correctly *enquest*, from the O. F. *enqueste*, enquiry, examination. In Robert of Brunne's Handlyng Synne, l. 5508, *quest* is used to translate the O. F. *enqueste*, with the sense of enquiry. 'The Frankish capitularies had a process called *inquisitio*, which was adopted into Norman law, and was there called *enquête* [in true old spelling *enqueste*] : this, having passed with the Normans into England, was finally shaped and embodied in the common law among the legal reforms of Henry II ;' Earle, Anglo-Saxon Literature, p. 165.

816. For the second *it* read *him*.

850. Perhaps read—And Gamelyn cleuede ·[a-two] his cheeke-boon.

871. Wyclif complains that 'iurrouris in questis wolen for-sweren hem [*forswear themselves*] wittyngly for here dyner and a noble ;' Works, ed. Matthew, p. 183.

THE TALE OF GAMELYN.

LITHETH, and lesteneth · and herkeneth aright,
　　And ȝe schulle here a talkyng · of a doughty knight;
Sire Iohan of Boundys · was his righte name,
He cowde of norture ynough · and mochil of game.
Thre sones the knight hadde · that with his body he wan;　5
The eldest was a moche schrewe · and sone he bygan.
His bretheren loued wel here fader · and of him were agast,
The eldest deserued his fadres curs · and had it at the last.
The goode knight his fader · lyuede so ȝore,
That deth was comen him to · and handled him ful sore.　10
The goode knight cared sore · sik ther he lay,
How his children scholde · lyuen after his day.
He hadde ben wyde-wher · but non housbond he was,
Al the lond that he hadde · it was verrey purchas.
Fayn he wolde it were · dressed among hem alle,　15

N.B.—Hl. = Harleian MS. no. 7334 (*taken as the foundation of the text*); Harl. (1758) = Harleian MS. no. 1758; Cp. = MS. Corp. Chr. Coll. Oxford; Ln. = Lansdowne MS. no. 851; Pt. = Petworth MS.; Rl. = MS. Royal 18 c. ii; Sl. = MS. Sloane, no. 1685.

1. Cp. lesteneth; Sl. Ln. listeneth; Hl. lestneth. Cp. herkeneth; Rl. Sl. herkenyth; Hl. herkneth. 2. Cp. schulle; Ln. schullen; Hl. schul. Hl. heere; Cp. heeren; *the rest* here. 3. Hl. right (*which the rest omit*); *read* righte. 4. Hl. ynough; *the rest omit.* 5. Cp. hadde; Rl. Sl. Pt. Ln. had; Hl. *omits.* 7. Pt. brether. 8. Cp. hadde (*which seems better*). 14. Cp. Rl. hadde; Hl. had (*and in l.* 16). 15. Cp. Ln. wolde; Hl. wold. Ln. y-dressed. Hl. amonges; *the rest* among; *see l.* 36.

That ech of hem hadde his part · as it mighte falle.
Tho sente he in-to cuntre · after wise knightes,
To helpe delen his londes · and dressen hem to-rightes.
He sente hem word by lettres · they schulden hye blyue,
Yf they wolde speke with him · whil he was on lyue.　　　　20
　　Tho the knyghtes herden · sik that he lay,
Hadde they no reste · nother night ne day,
Til they comen to him · ther he lay stille
On his deth-bedde · to abyde goddes wille.
Than seyde the goode knight · syk ther he lay,　　　　25
'Lordes, I you warne · for soth, withoute nay,
I may no lenger lyuen · heer in this stounde;
For thurgh goddes wille · deth draweth me to grounde.'
Ther nas non of hem alle · that herde him aright,
That they ne hadden reuthe · of that ilke knight,　　　　30
And seyde, ' sir, for goddes loue · ne dismay ȝou nought;
God may do bote of bale · that is now i-wrought.'
　　Than spak the goode knight · sik ther he lay,
' Boote of bale god may sende · I wot it is no nay;
But I byseke ȝou, kniȝtes · for the loue of me,　　　　35
Goth and dresseth my lond · among my sones thre.
And for the loue of god · deleth hem nat amys,
And forgetith nat Gamelyn · my ȝonge sone that is.
Taketh heed to that on · as wel as to that other ;
Selde ȝe see ony eyr · helpen his brother.'　　　　40
　　Tho lete they the knight lyen · that was nought in hele,
And wenten in-to counseil · his landes for to dele ;

16. Hl. might.　　17. Cp. Sl. Rl. Pt. Ln. sente ; Hl. sent. *So in*
l. 19, *where the* MSS. *wrongly have* sent.　　21. Hl. ther ; *but all the*
rest that.　　24. Pt. dethes bedde.　　27. Hl. Cp. lengere ; Ln.
longer ; *the rest* lenger.　　29. Sl. Cp. Ln. herde ; Hl. herd.　　30. Harl.
(1758) Pt. ne ; *which the rest wrongly omit.*　　31. Cp. Pt. *om.* ne.
37. Ill. And sires ; *but the rest omit* sires.　　41. Hl. leete ; Ft. Ln.
lete ; *the rest* leten, leeten.

For to delen hem alle · to oon, that was her thought,
And for Gamelyn was ȝongest · he schulde haue nought.
Al the lond that ther was · they dalten it in two,   45
And leten Gamelyn the ȝonge · withoute londe go,
And ech of hem seyde · to other ful lowde,
His bretheren might ȝeue him lond · whan he good cowde.
Whan they hadde deled · the lond at here wille,
They comen to the knight · ther he lay ful stille,   50
And tolden him anon · how they hadden wrought;
And the knight ther he lay · liked it right nought.
Than seyde the knight · 'by seynt Martyn,
For al that ȝe haue y-doon · yit is the lond myn;
For goddes loue, neyhebours · stondeth alle stille,   55
And I wil dele my lond · right after my wille.
Iohan, myn eldeste sone · schal haue plowes fyue,
That was my fadres heritage · whil he was on lyue;
And my myddeleste sone · fyue plowes of lond,
That I halp for to gete · with my righte hond;   60
And al myn other purchas · of londes and of leedes,
That I byquethe Gamelyn · and alle my goode steedes.
And I byseke ȝow, goode men · that lawe conne of londe,
For Gamelynes loue · that my queste stonde.'
Thus dalte the knight · his lond by his day,   65
Right on his deth-bedde · sik ther he lay;
And sone aftirward · he lay stoon-stille,
And deyde whan tyme com · as it was Cristes wille.

44. Hl. schuld; Cp. scholde.   46. Hl. Cp. leeten; Rl. Sl. Ln. leten. Pt. londe; Ln. lande; *the rest* lond.   48. Cp. mowe; Ln. mow; *read* mighte.   50. Hl. come aȝein; *but the rest omit* aȝein, *and read* comen, camen, commen.   51. Hl. anon right; *the rest* anon, anoon. 54. Hl. y-doon; *the rest* don, done.   56. Hl. Pt. *om.* right; *the rest have it.*   59. Hl. fyf; *the rest* fyue; *see l.* 57.   60. *Read* righte; *yet the* MSS. *have* right.   61. Ln. of ledes; *the rest omit* 2nd of. 64. Cp. bequeste.   66. Hl. bed; Cp. bedde; *see l.* 24.

Anon as he was deed · and vnder gras i-graue,
Sone the elder brother · gyled the ȝonge knaue;   70
He took into his hond · his lond and his leede,
And Gamelyn himselfe · to clothen and to feede.
He clothed him and fedde him · yuel and eek wrothe,
And leet his londes for-fare · and his houses bothe,
His parkes and his woodes · and dede nothing wel;   75
And seththen he it aboughte · on his faire fel.
So longe was Gamelyn · in his brotheres hallé,
For the strengest, of good wil · they doutiden him alle;
Ther was non ther-inne · nowther ȝong ne old,
That wolde wraththe Gamelyn · were he neuer so bold.   80
Gamelyn stood on a day · in his brotheres ȝerde,
And bygan with his hond · to handlen his berde;
He thoughte on his londes · that layen vnsawe,
And his faire okes · that down were i-drawe;
His parkes were i-broken · and his deer byreued;   85
Of alle his goode steedes · noon was him byleued;
His howses were vnhiled · and ful yuel dight;
Tho thoughte Gamelyn · it wente nought aright.
Afterward cam his brother · walkynge thare,
And seyde to Gamelyn · 'is our mete ȝare?'   90
Tho wraththed him Gamelyn · and swor by goddes book,
'Thou schalt go bake thi-self · I wil nought be thy cook!'
'How? brother Gamelyn · how answerest thou now?
Thou spake neuer such a word · as thou dost now.'
'By my faith,' seyde Gamelyn · 'now me thinketh neede,   95

---

69. Hl. And anon; *the rest omit* And.   71. Hl. as his
(*for* and his).   73. Hl. fed; *the rest* fedde.   76. Cp. aboughte;
Ln. abouhte; *the rest* abought, abowght.   79, 80. Rl. Sl. old, bold;
the rest olde, bolde.   83. Ln. þouhte; *the rest omit the final* e;
see l. 88.   85. Hl. byreeued (*see l.* 97); *the rest* reued, reuede.
87. Hl. Rl. Sl. Cp. vnhiled; Pt. vnhilled.

Of alle the harmes that I haue · I tok neuer ar heede.
My parkes ben to-broken · and my deer byreued,
Of myn armure and my steedes · nought is me bileued;
Al that my fader me byquath · al goth to schame,
And therfor haue thou goddes curs · brother by thy name!'
Than byspak his brother · that rape was of rees,   101
'Stond stille, gadelyng · and hold right thy pees;
Thou schalt be fayn for to haue · thy mete and thy wede ;
What spekest thou, Gamelyn · of lond other of leede?'
Thanne seyde Gamelyn · the child that was ying,   105
'Cristes curs mot he haue · that clepeth me gadelyng !
I am no worse gadelyng · ne no worse wight,
But born of a lady · and geten of a knight.'
Ne durste he nat to Gamelyn · ner a-foote go,
But clepide to him his men · and seyde to hem tho,   110
'Goth and beteth this boy · and reueth him his wyt,
And lat him lerne another tyme · to answere me bet.'
Thanne seyde the child · ȝonge Gamelyn,
'Cristes curs mot thou haue · brother art thou myn !
And if I schal algate · be beten anon,   115
Cristes curs mot thou haue · but thou be that oon!'
And anon his brother · in that grete hete
Made his men to fette staues · Gamelyn to bete.
Whan that euerich of hem · hadde a staf i-nome,
Gamelyn was war anon · tho he seigh hem come;   120
Tho Gamelyn seyh hem come · he loked ouer-al,
And was war of a pestel · stood vnder a wal;
Gamelyn was light of foot · and thider gan he lepe,
And drof alle his brotheres men · right sone on an hepe.

103. Rl. Sl. Pt. *om.* for.   109. Hl. durst ; Cp. durste ; Ln. dorste.
112. Cp. lere ; Hl. Ln. leren ; *the rest* lerne.   119. Hl. a staf had ;
the rest hadde (*or* had) a staf.   124. Hl. Ln. *om.* sone ; *the rest*
have it.

He loked as a wilde lyoun · and leyde on good woon ;   125
Tho his brother say that · he bigan to goon ;
He fley vp in-til a loft · and schette the dore fast ;
Thus Gamelyn with his pestel · made hem alle agast.
Some for Gamelynes loue · and some for his eyȝe,
Alle they drowe by halues · tho he gan to pleyȝe.   130
'What! how now ?' seyde Gamelyn · 'euel mot ȝe thee !
Wil ȝe bygynne contek · and so sone flee ?'
Gamelyn soughte his brother · whider he was flowe,
And saugh wher he loked · out at a wyndowe.
'Brother,' sayde Gamelyn · 'com a litel ner,   135
And I wil teche the a play · atte bokeler.'
His brother him answerde · and swor by seynt Rycher,
'Whil the pestel is in thin hond · I wil come no neer :
Brother, I wil make thy pees · I swere by Cristes ore ;
Cast away the pestel · and wraththe the nomore.'   140
'I mot neede,' sayde Gamelyn · 'wraththe me at oones,
For thou wolde make thy men · to breke myne boones,
Ne hadde I had mayn · and might in myn armes,
To haue i-put hem fro me · thei wolde haue do me harmes.'
'Gamelyn,' sayde his brother · 'be thou nought wroth,   145
For to seen the haue harm · it were me right loth ;
I ne dide it nought, brother · but for a fondyng,
For to loken if thou were strong · and art so ying.'
'Com a-doun than to me · and graunte me my bone
Of oo thing I wil the aske · and we schul saughte sone.'   150
Doun than cam his brother · that fykil was and fel,

128. *All but* Hl. *have* his ; Hl. the.   129, 130. Hl. eyȝe, pleyȝe ; *the rest* eye, pleye.   133. *The* MSS. *omit final* e *in* soughte, *as it is elided.*   143. Cp. hadde I had ; Hl. had I hadde.   144. Hl. he ; *the rest* thei.   148. Harl. (1758) Ln. if ; Pt. wher ; *the rest* or.   150. Hl. Cp. Ln. Of ; Harl. (1758) Of oo ; Rl. Of a ; Sl. Of o ; Pt. Of oon. 151, 152. Ln. fel, pestel ; *the rest* felle, pestelle.

And was swithe sore · agast of the pestel.
He seyde, 'brother Gamelyn · aske me thy boone,
And loke thou me blame · but I it graunte sone.'
Thanne seyde Gamelyn · 'brother, i-wys,   155
And we schulle ben at oon · thou most me graunte this:
Al that my fader me byquath · whil he was on lyue,
Thou most do me it haue · ʒif we schul nat stryue.'
'That schalt thou haue, Gamelyn · I swere by Cristes ore!
Al that thi fader the byquath · though thou woldest haue
    more;   160
Thy lond, that lyth laye · ful wel it schal be sowe,
And thyn howses reysed vp · that ben leyd so lowe.'
Thus seyde the knight · to Gamelyn with mowthe,
And thoughte eek on falsnes · as he wel couthe.
The knight thoughte on tresoun · and Gamelyn on noon, 165
And wente and kiste his brother · and, whan they were at
    oon,
Allas! ʒonge Gamelyn · nothing he ne wiste
With which a false tresoun · his brother him kiste!
    Litheth, and lesteneth · and holdeth your tonge,
And ye schul heere talkyng · of Gamelyn the yonge.   170
Ther was ther bysiden · cryed a wrastlyng,
And therfor ther was set vp · a ram and a ryng;
And Gamelyn was in wille · to wende therto,
For to preuen his might · what he cowthe do.

154. Hl. *om.* it; *the rest have it.*   161. Hl. Cp. laye; Rl. leie;
Sl. leye; Pt. Ln. ley.   164. Cp. þoughte; *the rest omit final* e.
Hl. Cp. Ln. of; *the rest* on; *see next line.*   165. *For* knight, Hl.
wrongly has king. *The MSS. omit final* e *in* thoughte.   166. Pt.
Hl. (1758) wente; *the rest* went. Hl. kist; *the rest* kissed; *but see*
l. 168.   169. Rl. lysteneth; Cp. lesteneth; Pt. listeneth; Hl. lest-
neth.   171. Hl. wrastlyng; Cp. wrasteling; Rl. wrastelynge;
Pt. wrastelinge.   172. Hl. sette (*wrongly*); *see l.* 184.   173.
Hl. good wil; Ln. wil; *the rest* wille.

'Brother,' seyde Gamelyn · 'by seynt Richer,   175
Thou most lene me to-nyght · a litel courser
That is freisch to the spores · on for to ryde;
I most on an erande · a litel her byside.'
'By god !' seyde his brother · 'of steedes in my stalle
Go and chese the the best · and spare non of alle   180
Of steedes or of coursers · that stonden hem bisyde;
And tel me, goode brother · whider thou wolt ryde.'
  'Her byside, brother · is cryed a wrastlyng,
And therfor schal be set vp · a ram and a ryng;
Moche worschip it were · brother, to vs alle,   185
Might I the ram and the ryng · bring home to this halle.'
A steede ther was sadeled · smertely and skeet;
Gamelyn did a paire spores · fast on his feet.
He sette his foot in the styrop · the steede he bystrood,
And toward the wrastelyng · the ȝonge child rood.   190
Tho Gamelyn the yonge · was riden out at gat,
The false kniȝt his brother · lokked it after that,
And bysoughte Iesu Crist · that is heuen kyng,
He mighte breke his nekke · in that wrastelyng.
As sone as Gamelyn com · ther the place was,   195
He lighte doun of his steede · and stood on the gras,
And ther he herd a frankeleyn · wayloway synge,
And bigan bitterly · his hondes for to wrynge.
'Goode man,' seyde Gamelyn · 'why makestow this fare ?
Is ther no man that may · ȝou helpe out of this care ?' 200

---

177. Hl. Pt. spore; *the rest* spores.   179. Hl. seyd; *the rest*
have final e.   181. *For* coursers, Hl. *wrongly has* course.   183.
Pt. wrasteling; Ln. warsteling; *the rest* wrastlyng *or* wrastlynge.   189.
Hl. set; Ln. sete; *the rest* sette.   191. Hl. ride; *the rest* riden, reden.
Hl. Ln. at the; Cp. Pt. atte; *the rest* at.   *All the* MSS. *have* gate
(*wrongly*); *and* thate (*for* that) *in the next line.*   192. Cp. Ln.
false; *the rest* fals.   194. Pt. wrestelinge; *the rest* wrastlyng, wrastlinge, wrestlinge.   197, 198. Hl. syng, wryng. Hl. hondos, *by mistake.*

'Allas!' seyde this frankeleyn · 'that euer was I bore!
For tweye stalworthe sones · I wene that I haue lore;
A champioun is in the place · that hath i-wrouȝt me sorwe,
For he hath slayn my two sones · but-if god hem borwe.
I wold ȝeue ten pound · by Iesu Crist! and more,   205
With the nones I fand a man · to handelen him sore.'
'Goode man,' sayde Gamelyn · 'wilt thou wel doon,
Hold myn hors, whil my man · draweth of my schoon,
And help my man to kepe · my clothes and my steede,
And I wil into place go · to loke if I may speede.'   210
'By god!' sayde the frankeleyn · 'anon it schal be doon;
I wil my-self be thy man · and drawen of thy schoon,
And wende thou into place · Iesu Crist the speede,
And drede not of thy clothes · nor of thy goode steede.'

  Barfoot and vngert · Gamelyn in cam,   215
Alle that weren in the place · heede of him they nam,
How he durste auntre him · of him to doon his might
That was so doughty champioun · in wrastlyng and in fight.
Vp sterte the champioun · rapely anoon,
Toward ȝonge Gamelyn · he bigan to goon,   220
And sayde, 'who is thy fader · and who is thy sire?
For sothe thou art a gret fool · that thou come hire!'
Gamelyn answerde · the champioun tho,
'Thou knewe wel my fader · whil he couthe go,
Whiles he was on lyue · by seint Martyn!   225
Sir Iohan of Boundys was his name · and I Gamelyn.'
'Felaw,' seyde the champioun · 'al-so mot I thryue,
I knew wel thy fader · whil he was on lyue;
And thiself, Gamelyn · I wil that thou it heere,
Whil thou were a ȝong boy · a moche schrewe thou were.' 230

205. Cp. handelen; Hl. handil.   213. Hl. Cp. Ln. the place; *the
rest omit* the; *see l.* 210.   217. Hl. Pt. durst; *the rest* durste, dorste.
219. Hl. raply and; *the rest* rapely, *omitting* and.

Than seyde Gamelyn · and swor by Cristes ore,
'Now I am older woxe · thou schalt me fynde a more!'
'Be god!' sayde the champioun · · 'welcome mote thou be!
Come thou ones in myn hond · schalt thou neuer the.'
It was wel withinne the night · and the moone schon,   235
Whan Gamelyn and the champioun · togider gonne goon.
The champioun caste tornes · to Gamelyn that was prest,
And Gamelyn stood stille · and bad him doon his best.
Thanne seyde Gamelyn · to the champioun,
'Thou art faste aboute · to brynge me adoun;   240
Now I haue i-proued · many tornes of thyne,
Thow most,' he seyde, 'prouen · on or tuo of myne.'
Gamelyn to the champioun · ȝede smertely anon,
Of all the tornes that he cowthe · he schewed him but oon,
And kaste him on the lefte syde · that thre ribbes tobrak, 245
And therto his oon arm · that ȝaf a gret crak.
Thanne seyde Gamelyn · smertely anoon,
'Schal it be holde for a cast · or elles for noon?'
'By god!' seyde the champioun · · 'whether that it bee,
He that cometh ones in thin hand · schal he neuer thee!' 250
Than seyde the frankeleyn · that had his sones there,
'Blessed be thou, Gamelyn · that euer thou bore were!'
The frankeleyn seyde to the champioun · of him stood him
     noon eye,
'This is yonge Gamelyn · that taughte the this pleye.'
Agein answerd the champioun · that liked nothing wel, 255

---

232. Hl. fynd; *the rest* fynde, finde.   236. Hl. gon to; Cp. Ln.
gonne; *the rest* gon.   243. Hl. Ln. smartly; Rl. Pt. smertely;
see l. 187.   245. *All have* kast *or* kest; *the e being elided.* MSS.
left, lift; *read* lefte.   247. Hl. smertly; *see l.* 243.   249,
253, 260. Hl. seyd; *the rest have final* e.   250. Hl. Ln. comes;
the rest cometh. *We should probably read*—That cometh ones. *omitting*
He.   255. Hl. welle; Cp. welle; *the rest* wel, well, welle.

' He is our alther mayster · and his pley is riȝt fel;
Sith I wrastled first · it is i-go ful ȝore,
But I was neuere in my lyf · handeled so sore.'
Gamelyn stood in the place · allone withoute serk,
And seyde, ' if ther be eny mo · lat hem come to werk ; 260
The champioun that peyned him · to werke so sore,
It semeth by his continaunce · that he wil nomore.'
Gamelyn in the place · stood as stille as stoon,
For to abyde wrastelyng · but ther com noon ;
Ther was noon with Gamelyn · wolde wrastle more, 265
For he handled the champioun · so wonderly sore.
Two gentil-men ther were · that yemede the place,
Comen to Gamelyn · (god ȝeue him goode grace!)
And sayde to him, ' do on · thyn hosen and thy schoon,
For sothe at this tyme · this feire is i-doon.' 270
And than seyde Gamelyn · ' so mot I wel fare,
I haue nought ȝet haluendel · sold vp my ware.'
Tho seyde the champioun · ' so brouke I my sweere,
He is a fool that therof byeth · thou sellest it so deere.'
Tho sayde the frankeleyn · that was in moche care, 275
' Felaw,' he seyde · ' why lakkest thou his ware ?
By seynt Iame in Galys · that many man hath sought, ✕
Ȝet it is to good cheep · that thou hast i-bought.'
Tho that wardeynes were · of that wrastelyng
Come and broughte Gamelyn · the ram and the ryng, 280
And seyden, ' haue, Gamelyn · the ryng and the ram,
For the beste wrasteler · that euer here cam.'

---

256. Cp. oure alther ; Hl. a lither (*corruptly*) ; *the rest* alther. *For*
fel, *the* MSS. *have* felle *or* felle.   258. Hl. Cp. Ln. *omit* in. Rl.
Pt. Ln. handeled ; Hl. Sl. Cp. handled.   273. Hl. brouk ; Cp. Ln.
brouke ; Pt. broke.   274. Hl. beyeth ; *the rest* byeth, bieth.   279.
Pt. wrasteling ; Ln. warstelinge ; Rl. wrastlinge ; *the rest* wrastlyng.
282. Cp. beste ; Hl. Ln. best ; *the rest omit ll.* 281, 282.

Thus wan Gamelyn · the ram and the ryng,
And wente with moche ioye · home in the mornyng.
His brother seih wher he cam · with the grete rowte,　285
And bad schitte the gate · and holde him withoute.
The porter of his lord · was ful sore agast,
And sterte anon to the gate · and lokked it fast.
　　Now litheth, and lesteneth · bothe ȝonge and olde,
And ȝe schul heere gamen · of Gamelyn the bolde.　.　290
Gamelyn come therto · for to haue comen in,
And thanne was it i-schet · faste with a pyn;
Than seyde Gamelyn · 'porter, vndo the yat,
For many good mannes sone · stondeth therat.'
Than answerd the porter · and swor by goddes berde,　295
' Thow ne schalt, Gamelyn · come into this ȝerde.'
' Thow lixt,' sayde Gamelyn · ' so browke I my chyn ! '
He smot the wyket with his foot · and brak awey the pyn.
The porter seyh tho · it might no better be,
He sette foot on erthe · and bigan to flee.　　　300
' By my faith,' seyde Gamelyn · ' that trauail is i-lore,
For I am of foot as light as thou · though thou haddest swore.'
Gamelyn ouertook the porter · and his teene wrak,
And gerte him in the nekke · that the bon to-brak,
And took him by that oon arm · and threw him in a welle,　305
Seuen fadmen it was deep · as I haue herd telle.
Whan Gamelyn the yonge · thus hadde pleyd his play,
Alle that in the ȝerde were · drewen hem away;
They dredden him ful sore · for werkes that he wrouȝte,
And for the faire company · that he thider broughte.　310

288. Rl. Harl. (1758) sterte ; *the rest* stert.　　　289. Hl. lestneth ;
Pt. listneþ ; *the rest* lesteneth, listenythe, listeneth, lysteneyth. Pt. Ln.
ȝonge ; *the rest* yong, ȝong.　　293. *The* MSS. *have* yate, gate ; *and
in the next line* therate.　　295. Hl. berd.　　300. Hl. Cp. he (*for
·and*) ; *the rest* and.　　304. Hl. Cp. gert ; *the rest* girt ; *the final e being
elided.*　　306. Hl. Cp. fadmen ; Pt. fadme ; Rl. Sl. fadame ; Ln. faþem.

Gamelyn ʒede to the gate · and leet it vp wyde;
He leet in alle maner men · that gon in wolde or ryde,
And seyde, 'ʒe be welcome · withouten eny greeue,
For we wiln be maistres heer · and aske no man leue.
ʒestirday I lefte ' · seyde ʒonge Gamelyn,   315
'In my brother seller · fyue tonne of wyn;
I wil not that this compaignye · parten a-twynne,
And ʒe wil doon after me · whil eny sope is thrynne;
And if my brother grucche · or make foul cheere,
Other for spense of mete or drynk · that we spenden heere, 320
I am oure catour · and bere oure aller purs,
He schal haue for his grucchyng · seint Maries curs.
My brother is a nyggoun · I swer by Cristes ore,
And we wil spende largely · that he hath spared ʒore;
And who that maketh grucchyng · that we here dwelle,   325
He schal to the porter · into the draw-welle.'
Seuen dayes and seuen nyght · Gamelyn held his feste,
With moche myrth and solas · was ther, and no cheste;
In a litel toret · his brother lay i-steke,
And sey hem wasten his good · but durste he not speke. 330
Erly on a mornyng · on the eighte day,
The gestes come to Gamelyn · and wolde gon here way.
'Lordes,' seyde Gamelyn · 'wil ye so hye?
Al the wyn is not ʒet dronke · so brouke I myn ye.'
Gamelyn in his herte · was he ful wo,   335
Whan his gestes took her leue · from him for to go;
He wold they had lenger abide · and they seyde nay,

312. Hl. Rl. Pt. wold; Cp. Ln. wolde.   318. Hl. thrynne; Cp. thrinne; Sl. Pt. þer-inne; Ln. þere-inne.   323. Hl. nyggoun; Rl. Sl. nygon; Pt. nigon; Cp. Ln. negon.   328. Hl. that was; *the rest omit* that (*which is rather to be understood than expressed*). 330. Hl. Cp. durst; *the rest* dorst; *the* e *being elided.*   334. Hl. y-dronke; *the rest omit* y-.   Pt. Ln. brouke; Rl. browke; Hl. brouk. 337. Hl. lenger abide; *the rest* dwelled lenger.

But bitaughte Gamelyn · god, and good day.
Thus made Gamelyn his feste · and brought it wel to ende,
And after his gestes · toke leue to wende.   340
  Litheth, and lesteneth · and holdeth youre tonge,
And ȝe schul heere gamen · of Gamelyn the ȝonge ;
Herkeneth, lordynges · and lesteneth aright,
Whan alle the gestes were goon · how Gamelyn was dight.
Al the whil that Gamelyn · heeld his mangerye,   345
His brother thoughte on him be wreke · with his treccherie.
Tho Gamelyns gestes · were riden and i-goon,
Gamelyn stood allone · frendes had he noon ;
Tho after ful soone · withinne a litel stounde,
Gamelyn was i-taken · and ful harde i-bounde.   350
Forth com the false knight · out of the selleer,
To Gamelyn his brother · he ȝede ful neer,
And sayde to Gamelyn · 'who made the so bold
For to stroye my stoor · of myn houshold ? '
'Brother,' seyde Gamelyn · 'wraththe the right nouȝt,   355
For it is many day i-gon · siththen it was bouȝt ;
For, brother, thou hast i-had · by seynt Richer,
Of fiftene plowes of lond · this sixtene yer,
And of alle the beestes · thou hast forth bred,
That my fader me biquath · on his dethes bed ;   360
Of al this sixtene ȝeer · I ȝeue the the prow,
For the mete and the drynk · that we have spended now.'
Thanne seyde the false knyȝt · (euel mot he the!)
'Herkne, brother Gamelyn · what I wol ȝeue the ;

339. Cp. feeste ; *the rest* fest, feest.   340. Hl. gestys ; *see l.* 336.
Hl. took ; Ln. had take ; Cp. toke ; Sl. to (*sic*) ; *the rest* toke.   341.
Hl. lestneth ; Pt. listen ; *the rest* lesteneth, listenyth.   343. Hl. herkneth ; *the rest* herkeneth, herkenyth, harkeneth.   346. MSS.
thought.   350. Hl. i-take ; *the rest* taken. Cp. Ln. harde ; *the rest*
hard.   351. Cp. Rl. Ln. false ; *the rest* fals.   360. Pt. dethes ;
the rest deth.   363. Rl. Sl. Cp. Ln. false ; *the rest* fals.

For of my body, brother · heir geten have I noon,   365
I wil make the myn heir · I swere by seint Iohan.'
'*Par ma foy!*' sayde Gamelyn · 'and if it so be,
And thou thenke as thou seyst · god ȝelde it the!'
Nothing wiste Gamelyn · of his brotheres gyle;
Therfore he him bigyled · in a litel while.   370
'Gamelyn,' seyde he · 'o thing I the telle;
Tho thou threwe my porter · in the draw-welle,
I swor in that wraththe · and in that grete moot,
That thou schuldest be bounde · bothe hand and foot;
Therfore I the biseche · brother Gamelyn,   375
Lat me nought be forsworen · brother art thou myn;
Lat me bynde the now · bothe hand and feet,
For to holde myn auow · as I the biheet.'
'Brother,' sayde Gamelyn · 'al-so mot I the!
Thou schalt not be forsworen · for the loue of me.'   380
Tho made they Gamelyn to sitte · mighte he nat stonde,
Tyl they hadde him bounde · bothe foot and honde.
The false knight his brother · of Gamelyn was agast,
And sente aftir feteres · to feteren him fast.
His brother made lesynges · on him ther he stood,   385
And tolde hem that comen in · that Gamelyn was wood.
Gamelyn stood to a post · bounden in the halle,
Tho that comen in ther · lokede on him alle.
Euer stood Gamelyn · euen vpright;
But mete ne drynk had he non · neither day ne night.   390
Than seyde Gamelyn · 'brother, by myn hals,

365. Hl. Cp. Ln. geten heir (heer, here); *the rest* heir (heire, here)
geten.   367. Hl. sayd; *the rest have final* e.   376. Hl. forsworn;
but see l. 380.   381. Hl. might; *but read* mighte; *the rest vary.*
382. Sl. Ln. hadde; Cp. hadden; *the rest* had, hadd.   383. Cp.
Ln. false; *the rest* fals.   384. Cp. sente; Sl. sende; *the rest* sent.
386. Hl. Rl. told; Ln. tolden; *the rest* tolde.   388. Cp. lokeden;
the rest loked; *but read* lokede.

Now I haue aspied · thou art a party fals;
Had I wist that tresoun · that thou haddest y-founde,
I wolde haue ȝeue the strokes · or I had be bounde!'
Gamelyn stood bounden · stille as eny stoon;　　　395
Two dayes and two nightes · mete had he noon.
Thanne seyde Gamelyn · that stood y-bounde stronge,
'Adam spenser · me thinkth I faste to longe;
Adam spenser · now I byseche the,
For the mochel loue · my fader loued the,　　　400
Yf thou may come to the keyes · lese me out of bond,
And I wil parte with the · of my free lond.'
Thanne seyde Adam · that was the spencer,
'I haue serued thy brother · this sixtene yeer,
If I leete the goon · out of his bour,　　　405
He wolde say afterward · I were a traytour.'
'Adam,' sayde Gamelyn · 'so brouke I myn hals!
Thou schalt fynde my brother · atte laste fals;
Therfor, brother Adam · louse me out of bond,
And I wil parte with the · of my free lond.'　　　410
'Vp swich a forward' · seyde Adam, 'i-wys,
I wil do therto · al·that in me is.'
'Adam,' seyde Gamelyn · 'al-so mot I the,
I wol holde the couenant · and thou wil lose me.'
Anon as Adames lord · to bedde was i-goon,　　　415
Adam took the keyes, and leet · Gamelyn out anoon;
He vnlokked Gamelyn · bothe handes and feet,
In hope of auauncement · that he him byheet.
Than seyde Gamelyn · 'thanked be goddes sonde!
Now I am loosed · bothe foot and honde;　　　420
Had I now eten · and dronken aright,

407. Hl. brouk; Cp. Pt. Ln. brouke.　　411. Hl. seyd; Rl. seid;
the rest add e.　　414. Hl. Sl. hold; *the rest* holde, halde. Cp.
lose; Harl. (1758) helpe; *the rest omit.*　　417. Hl. hand; Cp.
handes; *the rest* hondes.

Ther is noon in this hous · schuld bynde me this night.'
Adam took Gamelyn · as stille as ony stoon,
And ladde him in-to spence · rapely and anon,
And sette him to soper · right in a priue stede,   425
He bad him do gladly · and Gamelyn so dede.
Anon as Gamelyn hadde · eten wel and fyn,
And therto y-dronke wel · of the rede wyn,
'Adam,' seyde Gamelyn · 'what is now thy reed?
Wher I go to my brother · and girde of his heed?'   430
'Gamelyn,' seyde Adam · 'it schal not be so.
I can teche the a reed · that is worth the two.
I wot wel for sothe · that this is no nay,
We schul haue a mangery · right on Soneday;
Abbotes and priours · many heer schal be,   435
And other men of holy chirche · as I telle the;
Thow schalt stonde vp by the post · as thou were hond-fast,
And I schal leue hem vnloke · awey thou may hem cast.
Whan that they have eten · and wasschen here hondes,
Thou schalt biseke hem alle · to bryng the out of bondes; 440
And if they wille borwe the · that were good game,
Then were thou out of prisoun · and I out of blame;
And if euerich of hem · say vnto vs nay,
I schal do an other · I swere by this day!
Thou schalt haue a good staf · and I wil haue another,   445
And Cristes curs haue that oon · that faileth that other!'
'3e, for gode!' sayde Gamelyn · 'I say it for me,
If I fayle on my syde · yuel mot I the!
If we schul algate · assoile hem of here synne,

424. Hl. Cp. rapely and; *the rest omit* and.   430. Hl. Wher;
Ln. Where; Cp. For; *the rest* Or.   431. Hl. seyd; Sl. seid; *the
rest add* e.   434. Ln. sonondaye; Hl. *and the rest* sonday; *we should
read* sonnenday *or* soneday.   437. Pt. Ln. Harl. (1758) bounde
fast; *the rest* hond-fast (*rightly*).   439. Hl. waisschen; *the rest*
wasschen, wasshen.

Warne me, brother Adam · whan I schal bygynne.'   450
'Gamelyn,' seyde Adam · · 'by seynte Charite,
I wil warne the byforn · whan that it schal be;
Whan I twynke on the · loke for to goon,
And cast awey the feteres · and com to me anoon.'
'Adam,' seide Gamelyn · · 'blessed be thy bones !   455
That is a good counseil · ȝeuen for the nones;
If they werne me thanne · to brynge me out of bendes,
I wol sette goode strokes · right on here lendes.'
    Tho the Sonday was i-come · and folk to the feste,
Faire they were welcomed · bothe leste and meste;   460
And euer as they atte halle · dore comen in,
They caste their eye · on ȝonge Gamelyn.
The false knight his brother · ful of trechery,
Alle the gestes that ther were · atte mangery,
Of Gamelyn his brother · he tolde hem with mouthe   465
Al the harm and the schame · that he telle couthe.
Tho they were serued · of messes tuo or thre,
Than seyde Gamelyn · · 'how serue ȝe me?
It is nouȝt wel serued · by god that al made !
That I sytte fastyng · and other men make glade.'   470
The false knight his brother · ther that he stood,
Tolde alle his gestes · that Gamelyn was wood;
And Gamelyn stood stille · and answerde nought,
But Adames wordes · he held in his thought.
Tho Gamelyn gan speke · dolfully with-alle   475
To the grete lordes · that saten in the halle:
'Lordes,' he seyde · · 'for Cristes passioun,

450. Hl. I; *the rest* we.   453. Ln. twynke; Hl. Cp. twynk; *the rest* wynke, winke, wynk.   456. Hl. ȝeuyng; Cp. yeuyng; *the rest* yeuen, ȝeuen, *or* ȝiuen.   460. Hl. lest; Cp. leste.   463. Cp. Ln. false; *the rest* fals.   464. Hl. mangrery (*sic*).   467. Hl. other (*for* or).   471. Ln. false; *the rest* fals.

Helpeth brynge Gamelyn • out of prisoun.'
Than seyde an abbot • sorwe on his cheeke!
'He schal haue Cristes curs • and seynte Maries eeke,   480
That the out of prisoun • beggeth other borwe,
But euer worthe hem wel • that doth the moche sorwe.'
After that abbot • than spak another,
'I wold thin heed were of • though thou were my brother!
Alle that the borwe • foule mot hem falle !'   485
Thus they seyden alle • that weren in the halle.
Than seyde a priour • yuel mot he thryue !
'It is moche skathe, boy • that thou art on lyve.'
'Ow !' seyde Gamelyn • 'so brouke I my bon !
Now I have aspyed • that freendes have I non.   490
Cursed mot he worthe • bothe fleisch and blood,
That euer do priour • or abbot ony good !'
Adam the spencer • took vp the cloth,
And loked on Gamelyn • and say that he was wroth ;
Adam on the pantrye • litel he thoughte,   495
But tuo goode staues • to halle-dore he broughte,
Adam loked on Gamelyn • and he was war anoon,
And caste awey the feteres • and he bigan to goon :
Tho he com to Adam • he took that oo staf,
And bygan to worche • and goode strokes ʒaf.   500
Gamelyn cam in-to the halle • and the spencer bothe,
And loked hem aboute • as they had be wrothe ;
Gamelyn sprengeth holy-water • with an oken spire,
That some that stoode vpright • fellen in the fire.
There was no lewed man • that in the halle stood,   505

486. Hl. seyde; Pt. Ln. Harl. (1758) seiden. Hl. were; Cp. Ln.
weren.   489. Hl. brouk; *the rest* brouke, browke, broke.
495, 496. *The* MSS. *have* thought, brought; *against grammar.*   498.
Ln. keste; *the rest* cast.   504. Ln. fellen; *the rest* felle, fell.   505.
Hl. lewede; Pt. Ln. lewe; *the rest* lewed, lewid.

That wolde do Gamelyn · eny thing but good,
But stoode besyden · and leet hem bothe werche,
For they hadde no rewthe · of men of holy cherche;
Abbot or priour · monk or chanoun,
That Gamelyn ouertok · anon they ʒeeden doun.   510
Ther was non of hem alle · that with his staf mette,
That he ne made him overthrowe · and quitte him his dette.
'Gamelyn,' seyde Adam · 'for seynte Charite,
Pay large lyuerey · for the loue of me,
And I wil kepe the dore · so euer here I masse!   515
Er they ben assoyled · there shal noon passe.'
'Dowt the nought,' seyde Gamelyn · ' whil we ben in-feere,
Kep thou wel the dore · and I wol werche heere;
Stere the, good Adam · and lat ther noon flee,
And we schul telle largely · how many ther be.'   520
'Gamelyn,' seyde Adam · ' do hem but good;
They ben men of holy chirche · draw of hem no blood,
Saue wel the croune · and do hem non harmes,
But brek bothe her legges · and siththen here armes.'
Thus Gamelyn and Adam · wroughte right fast,   525
And pleyden with the monkes · and made hem agast.
Thider they come rydyng · iolily with swaynes,
And hom aʒen they were i-lad · in cartes and in waynes.
Tho they hadden al y-don · than seyde a gray frere,
' Allas! sire abbot · what dide we now heere?   530
Tho that we comen hider · it was a cold reed,
Vs hadde ben better at home · with water and with breede.'
Whil Gamelyn made ordres · of monkes and frere,
Euer stood his brother · and made foul chere;
Gamelyn vp with his staf · that he wel knew,   535

507. Hl. besyde; Rl. by-siden; Sl. bisiden; Cp. besyden.   512. Pt. Ln. ne; *which the rest omit.* Sl. Cp. quitte; Hl. quyt. Hl. him; *the rest* hem.   516. Hl. shan; *the rest* shal *or* schal.   530. Hl. did; Sl. Cp. Harl. (1758) dide.   531. Hl. *om.* we.   532. Hl. Pt. Ln. *om. second* with.

And gerte him in the nekke · that he ouerthrew;
A litel aboue the girdel · the rigge-bon to-barst;
And sette him in the feteres · ther he sat arst.
'Sitte ther, brother' · sayde Gamelyn,
'For to colen thy blood · as I dide myn.'   540
As swithe as they hadde · i-wroken hem on here foon,
They askeden watir · and wisschen anoon,
What some for here loue · and some for here awe,
Alle the seruantz serued hem · of the beste lawe.
The scherreue was thennes · but a fyue myle,   545
And al was y-told him · in a litel while,
How Gamelyn and Adam · had doon a sory rees,
Bounden and i-wounded men · aȝein the kinges pees;
Tho bigan sone · strif for to wake,
And the scherref was aboute · Gamelyn for to take.   550
　　Now lytheth and lesteneth · so god ȝif ȝou good fyn!
And ȝe schul heere good game · of ȝonge Gamelyn.
Four and twenty ȝonge men · that heelden hem ful bolde,
Come to the schirref · and seyde that they wolde
Gamelyn and Adam · fetten, by here fay;   555
The scherref ȝaf hem leue · soth as I ȝou say;
They hyeden faste · wold they nought bylynne,
Til they come to the gate · ther Gamelyn was inne.
They knokked on the gate · the porter was ny,
And loked out at an hol · as man that was sly.   560
The porter hadde byholde · hem a litel while,
He loued wel Gamelyn · and was adrad of gyle,
And leet the wicket stonden · y-steke ful stille,

---

536. Cp. gerte; *the rest* gert, girt, gerd.   540. Hl. colyn; Cp. coole;
Ln. coly; *the rest* colen.   543. Rl. Sl. Pt. Harl. (1758) *insert* her (here)
before awe; *which* Hl. Cp. Ln. *omit.*   550. *The two* Cambridge MSS.
have come; *rest om.; read* was; *cf.* 270, 285.   551. Hl. lestneth; Cp.
lesteneth; Hl. goode.   555. Rl. Sl. Pt. Harl. (1758) by her (here)
fay; Cp. be way; Hl. Ln. away.

And asked hem withoute • what was here wille.
For al the grete company • thanne spak but oon,   565
'Vndo the gate, porter • and lat vs in goon.'
Than seyde the porter • ' so brouke I my chyn,
ȝe schul sey your erand • er ȝe comen in.'
' Sey to Gamelyn and Adam • if here wille be,
We wil speke with hem • wordes two or thre.'   570
' Felaw,' seyde the porter • 'stond there stille,
And I wil wende to Gamelyn • to witen his wille.'
In wente the porter • to Gamelyn anoon,
And seyde, ' Sir, I warne ȝou • her ben come ȝour foon;
The scherreues meyne • ben atte gate,   575
For to take ȝou bothe • schulle ȝe nat skape.'
' Porter,' seyde Gamelyn • ' so moot I wel the !
I wil allowe the thy wordes • whan I my tyme se;
Go agayn to the ȝate • and dwel with hem a while,
And thou schalt se right sone • porter, a gyle.   580
Adam,' sayde Gamelyn • ' looke the to goon;
We have foomen atte gate • and frendes neuer oon;
It ben the schirrefes men • that hider ben i-come,
They ben swore to-gidere • that we schul be nome.'
' Gamelyn,' seyde Adam • ' hye the right blyue,   585
And if I faile the this day • euel mot I thryue !
And we schul so welcome • the scherreues men,
That some of hem schul make • here beddes in the fen.'
Atte posterne-gate • Gamelyn out wente,
And a good cart-staf • in his hand he hente;   590
Adam hente sone • another gret staf
For to helpe Gamelyn • and goode strokes ȝaf.
Adam felde tweyne • and Gamelyn felde thre,

---

573. Cp. Ln. Harl. (1758) wente; *the rest* went.   576. Cp. schulle;
Hl schul. Hl. *has* na (*for* nat); *the rest* not, nouht.   588. Hl.
den; Pt. fenne; *the rest* fen.   589. Cp. Ln. wente; *the rest* went.

The other setten feet on erthe · and bygonne fle.
'What?' seyde Adam · 'so euer here I masse!   595
I haue a draught of good wyn! · drynk er ye passe!'
'Nay, by god!' sayde thay · 'thy drynk is not good,
It wolde make a mannes brayn · to lien in his hood.'
Gamelyn stood stille · and loked him aboute,
And seih the scherreue come · with a gret route.   600
'Adam,' seyde Gamelyn · 'what be now thy reedes?
Here cometh the scherreue · and wil haue oure heedes.'
Adam seyde, 'Gamelyn · my reed is now this,
Abide we no lenger · lest we fare amys:
I rede that we to wode goon · ar that we be founde,   605
Better is vs ther loos · than in town y-bounde.'
Adam took by the hond · 3onge Gamelyn;
And euerich of hem tuo · drank a draught of wyn,
And after took her cours · and wenten her way;
Tho fond the scherreue · nest, but non ay.   610
The scherreue lighte adoun · and went in-to the halle,
And fond the lord y-fetered · faste with-alle.
The scherreue vnfetered him · sone, and that anoon,
And sente after a leche · to hele his rigge-boon.

Lete we now this false knight · lyen in his care,   615
And talke we of Gamelyn · and loke how he fare.
Gamelyn in-to the woode · stalkede stille,
And Adam the spenser · likede ful ylle;
Adam swor to Gamelyn · by seynt Richer,
'Now I see it is mery · to be a spencer,   620
That leuer me were · keyes for to bere,
Than walken in this wilde woode · my clothes to tere.'

598. Cp. Pt. Harl. (1758) a; *which the rest omit.* Hl. Ln. brayne;
the rest brayn.   602. Hl. comth; *the rest* cometh.   609. Hl. coursers;
rest cours; *see* ll. 617, 622.   614. Hl. sent; Cp. Sl. sente.   615. Cp.
Ln. false; *the rest* fals.   618. Cp. likede; Ln. loked; *the rest* liked.

'Adam,' seyde Gamelyn · 'dismaye the right nought;
Many good mannes child · in care is i-brought.'
And as they stoode talkyng · bothen in-feere,　　　　625
Adam herd talkyng of men · and neyh him thought thei were.
Tho Gamelyn vnder the woode · lokede aright,
Seuene score of ȝonge men · he saugh wel a-dight;
Alle satte atte mete · compas aboute.
'Adam,' seyde Gamelyn · 'now haue we no doute,　　　　630
After bale cometh boote · thurgh grace of god almight;
Me thynketh of mete and drynk · that I haue a sight.'
Adam lokede tho · vnder woode-bowȝ,
And whan he seyh mete · he was glad ynough;
For he hopede to god · for to haue his deel,　　　　635
And he was sore alonged · after a good meel.
As he seyde that word · the mayster outlawe
Saugh Gamelyn and Adam · vnder woode-schawe.
'Ȝonge men,' seyde the maister · 'by the goode roode,
I am war of gestes · god sende vs non but goode;　　　　640
Ȝonder ben tuo ȝonge men · wonder wel adight,
And parauenture ther ben mo · who so lokede aright.
Ariseth vp, ȝe ȝonge men · and fetteth hem to me;
It is good that we witen · what men they bee.'
Vp ther sterten seuene · fro the dyner,　　　　645
And metten with Gamelyn · and Adam spenser.
Whan they were neyh hem · than seyde that oon,
'Ȝeldeth vp, ȝonge men · ȝour bowes and ȝour floon.'
Thanne seyde Gamelyn · that ȝong was of elde,
'Moche sorwe mot he haue · that to ȝou hem yelde!　　　　650
I curse non other · but right my-selue;
They ȝe fette to ȝow fyue · thanne ȝe be twelue!'

627, 642. Hl. loked.　　　640. Cp. Pt. Harl. (1758) sende; *the rest*
send. Hl. non but; *which the rest omit.*　　　652. Hl. Cp. They; RL
Thei; Sl. Ln. Though.

Tho they herde by his word · that might was in his arm,
Ther was non of hem alle · that wolde do him harm,
But sayde vnto Gamelyn · myldely and stille,   655
' Com afore our maister · and sey to him thy wille.'
' Yonge men,' sayde Gamelyn · ' by ʒour lewte,
What man is ʒour maister · that ʒe with be?'
Alle they answerde · withoute lesyng,
' Oure maister is i-crouned · of outlawes kyng.'   660
' Adam,' seyde Gamelyn · ' gowe in Cristes name ;
He may neyther mete nor drynk · werne vs, for schame.
If that he be hende · and come of gentil blood,
He wol ʒeue vs mete and drynk · and doon vs som good.' ·
' By seynt Iame l' seyde Adam · ' what harm that I gete,   665
I wil auntre to the dore · that I hadde mete.'
Gamelyn and Adam · wente forth in-feere,
And they grette the maister · that they founde there.
Than seide the maister · kyng of outlawes,
' What seeke ʒe, ʒonge men · vnder woode-schawes?'   670
Gamelyn answerde · the kyng with his croune,
' He moste needes walke in woode · that may not walke in towne.
Sire, we walke not heer · noon harm for to do,
But if we meete with a deer · to scheete therto,
As men that ben hungry · and mow no mete fynde,   675
And ben harde bystad · vnder woode-lynde.'
Of Gamelynes wordes · the maister hadde routhe,
And seyde, ' ʒe schal haue ynough · haue god my trouthe ! '
He bad hem sitte ther adoun · for to take reste ;
And bad hem ete and drynke · and that of the beste.   680
As they sete and eeten · and dronke wel and fyn,

655. Hl. sayd ; *the rest add* e.   663. Hl. heende ; Cp. kynde ; *the rest*
hende.   664. Hl. an (*for* and).   665. Hl. seyd ; Ln. seid ; *the rest*
add e.   666. Hl. auntre ; *the rest* auenture me. Hl. Cp. Ln. to the
dore ; *which the rest omit.*

Than seyde that oon to that other · 'this is Gamelyn.'
Tho was the maister outlawe · in-to counseil nome,
And told how it was Gamelyn · that thider was i-come.
Anon as he herde · how it was bifalle,   685
He made him maister vnder him · ouer hem alle.
Within the thridde wyke · him com tydyng,
To the maister outlawe · that tho was her kyng,
That he schulde come hom · his pees was i-mad;
And of that goode tydyng · he was tho ful glad.   690
Tho seyde he to his ȝonge men · soth for to telle,
'Me ben comen tydynges · I may no lenger dwelle.'
Tho was Gamelyn anon · withoute taryyng,
Maad maister outlawe · and crouned here kyng.

Tho was Gamelyn crouned · kyng of outlawes,   695
And walked a while · vnder woode-schawes.
The false knight his brother · was scherreue and sire,
And leet his brother endite · for hate and for ire.
Tho were his bonde-men · sory and nothing glad,
When Gamelyn her lord · wolues-heed was cryed and maad;
And sente out of his men · wher they might him fynde,   701
For to seke Gamelyn · vnder woode-lynde,
To telle him tydynges · how the wynd was went,
And al his good reued · and alle his men schent.

Whan they had him founde · on knees they hem sette,   705
And a-doun with here hood · and here lord grette;
'Sire, wraththe ȝou nought · for the goode roode,
For we haue brought ȝou tydynges · but they be nat goode.
Now is thy brother scherreue · and hath the baillye,

682. Hl. seyd; *the rest add* e.   689. Hl. i-made; Cp. Sl. maad;
the rest made.   694. Cp. Maad; *the rest* Made (*but there should be
no final* e). Cp. Ln. here; *the rest* her.   697. Cp. Ln. false; *the rest*
fals.   699. Rl. Sl. glad; *the rest* glade, gladde.   700. Sl. Cp.
maad; *the rest* made, maade.   704. Hl. Cp. Ln. *omit* alle.

And he hath endited the · and wolues-heed doth the crie.'   710
'Allas !' seyde Gamelyn · 'that euer I was so slak
That I ne hadde broke his nekke · tho I his rigge brak !
Goth, greteth hem wel · myn housbondes and wyf,
I wol ben atte nexte schire · haue god my lyf !'
Gamelyn came wel redy · to the nexte schire,   715
And ther was his brother · bothe lord and sire.
Gamelyn com boldelych · in-to the moot-halle,
And put a-doun his hood · among the lordes alle ;
'God saue you alle, lordynges · that now here be !
But broke-bak scherreue · euel mot thou the !   720
Why hast thou do me · that schame and vilonye,
For to late endite me · and wolues-heed me crye ?'
Tho thoughte the false knight · for to ben awreke,
And leet take Gamelyn · moste he no more speke ;
Might ther be no more grace · but Gamelyn atte laste   725
Was cast in-to prisoun · and fetered ful faste.
Gamelyn hath a brother · that highte sir Ote,
As good a knight and hende · as mighte gon on foote.
Anon ther ȝede a messager · to that goode knight,
And tolde him altogidere · how Gamelyn was dight.   730
Anon as sire Ote herde · how Gamelyn was a-dight,
He was wonder sory · was he no-thing light,
And leet sadle a steede · and the way he nam,
And to his tweyne bretheren · anon-right he cam.
'Sire,' seyde sire Ote · to the scherreue tho,   735
'We ben but thre bretheren · schul we neuer be mo ;

712. Hl. *om. second* I ; *the rest have it.*   713. Hl. hem ; *which the rest omit.* *For* myn housbondes Harl. (1758) *has* boþe housbonde ; *which seems better.*   723. Cp. thoughte the false ; *the rest* thought the fals.   724. *The* MSS. *have* most, *the* e *being elided.*   725, 726. Rl. Sl. Cp. laste, faste ; *the rest* last, fast.   728. Hl. Cp. heende ; *the rest* hende.   730. Hl. Cp. told ; *the rest* tolde.   734. Hl. anon right ; Ln. ful sone ; *the rest* right sone.

And thou hast y-prisoned · the beste of us alle;
Swich another brother · yuel mot him bifalle!'
'Sire Ote,' seide the false knight · 'lát be thi curs;
By god, for thy wordes · he schal fare the wurs;   740
To the kynges prisoun · anon he is y-nome,
And ther he schal abyde · til the Iustice come.'
'Pardel!' seyde sir Ote · 'better it schal be;
I bidde him to maynpris · that thow graunte him me
Til the nexte sittyng · of delyueraunce,   745
And thanne lat Gamelyn · stande to his chaunce.'
'Brother, in swich a forward · I take him to the;
And by thi fader soule · that the bygat and me,
But if he be redy · whan the Iustice sitte,
Thou schalt bere the Iuggement · for al thi grete witte.' 750
'I graunte wel,' seide sir Ote · 'that it so be.
Let delyuer him anon · and tak him to me.'
Tho was Gamelyn delyuered · to sire Ote his brother;
And that night dwellede · that on with that other.
On the morn seyde Gamelyn · to sire Ote the hende,   755
'Brother,' he seide, 'I moot · for sothe from the wende,
To loke how my ȝonge men · leden here lyf,
Whether they lyuen in ioie · or elles in stryf.'
'Be god!' seyde sire Ote · 'that is a cold reed,
Now I see that al the cark · schal fallen on myn heed;   760
For when the Iustice sitte · and thou be nought y-founde,
I schal anon be take · and in thy stede i-bounde.'
'Brother,' sayde Gamelyn · 'dismaye the nought,

737. Rl. Cp. beste; *the rest* best.   739. Pt. Ln. false; *the rest* fals.   744. Hl. Cp. maymp*r*is. Hl. Sl. Ln. graunt; *the rest* graunte. Hl. him; Cp. Ln. to; *the rest omit.*   747. Hl. forthward; *the rest* forward.   754. Hl. Cp. dwelleden; Ln. dwelden; *the rest* dwellide, dwellid, dwelled.   755. Hl. Cp. heende; Rl. hynde; *the rest* hende. 761, 766. *The MSS. rightly have* sitte, *except that* Hl. *has* sitt *in l.* 766. *For* sitte (*like* be) *is in the subj. mood.*

For by seint Iame in Gales · that many man hath sought,
If that god almighty · holde my lyf and witte,　　765
I wil be ther redy · whan the Iustice sitte.'
Than seide sir Ote to Gamelyn · 'god schilde the fro schame;
Com whan thou seest tyme · and bring vs out of blame.'
　　Litheth, and lesteneth · and holdeth ȝou stille,
And ȝe schul here how Gamelyn · hadde al his wille.　　770
Gamelyn wente aȝein · vnder woode-rys,
And fond there pleying · ȝonge men of prys.
Tho was ȝong Gamelyn · glad and blithe ynough,
Whan he fond his mery men · vnder woode-bough.
Gamelyn and his men · talkeden in-feere,　　775
And they hadde good game · here maister to heere ;
They tolden him of auentures · that they hadde founde,
And Gamelyn hem tolde aȝein · how he was fast i-bounde.
Whil Gamelyn was outlawed · hadde he no cors ;
There was no man that for him · ferde the wors,　　780
But abbotes and priours · monk and chanoun ;
On hem left he no-thing · whan he mighte hem nom.
Whil Gamelyn and his men · made merthes ryue,
The false knight his brother · yuel mot he thryue !
For he was fast aboute · bothe day and other,　　785
For to hyre the quest · to hangen his brother.
Gamelyn stood on a day · and, as he biheeld
The woodes and the schawes · in the wilde feeld,
He thoughte on his brother · how he him beheet
That he wolde be redy · whan the Iustice seet ;　　790

765. Hl. hold; Rl. hold me ; *the rest* holde me.　　765, 766. Hl.
witt, sitt.　　769. Hl. lestneth ; Cp. lesteneth ; Rl. Pt. listeneth.　　770.
Rl. Sl. Cp. hadde ; *the rest* had.　　771. Cp. Sl. wente ; Hl. went.
775. Hl. talked ; Rl. Pt. talkeden ; Sl. talkiden.　　779. Sl. Cp. Ln.
hadde ; Rl. hade ; *the rest* had.　　782. *The* MSS. *have* might ;
the e *being elided.*　　784. Cp. false ; *the rest* fals.　　789. Hl.
thought ; *but see* l. 791.

He thoughte wel that he wolde • withoute delay,
Come afore the Iustice • to kepen his day,
And seide to his ȝonge men • ' dighteth ȝou ȝare,
For whan the Iustice sitte • we moote be thare,
For I am vnder borwe • til that I come,   795
And my brother for me • to prisoun schal be nome.'
' By seint Iame !' seyde his ȝonge men • ' and thou rede therto,
Ordeyne how it schal be • and it shall be do.'
Whil Gamelyn was comyng • ther the Iustice sat,
The false knight his brother • forȝat he nat that,   800
To huyre the men on his quest • to hangen his brother;
Though he hadde nought that oon • he wolde haue that other.
Tho cam Gamelyn • fro vnder woode-rys,
And broughte with him • his ȝonge men of prys.
    ' I se wel,' seyde Gamelyn • ' the Iustice is set;   805
Go aforn, Adam • and loke how it spet.'
Adam wente into the halle • and loked al aboute,
He seyh there stonde • lordes grete and stoute,
And sir Ote his brother • fetered wel fast;
Tho went Adam out of halle • as he were agast.   810
Adam said to Gamelyn • and to his felawes alle,
' Sir Ote stant i-fetered • in the moot-halle.'
' ȝonge men,' seide Gamelyn • ' this ȝe heeren alle;
Sire Ote stant i-fetered • in the moot-halle.'
If god ȝif vs grace • wel for to doo,   815
He schal it abegge • that broughte it thertoo.'
Thanne sayde Adam • that lokkes hadde hore,
' Cristes curs mote he haue • that him bond so sore !

794. Hl. sitt.   800. Cp. Ln. false; *the rest* fals.   805, 806.
MSS. sette, spette (*wrongly*).   807. Cp. wente; *the rest* went.
808. Cp. bothe grete; *rest om.* bothe. Hl. gret; *the rest* grete.   811.
Hl. felaws; *the rest* felawes, felowes.   816. Hl. *om. second* it.
818. Rl. Sl. Pt. mote ; Ln. mot; Hl. Cp. most.

And thou wilt, Gamelyn • do after my reed,
Ther is noon in the halle • schal bere awey his heed.'   820
'Adam,' seyde Gamelyn • 'we wiln nought don so,
We wil slee the giltyf • and lat the other go.
I wil into the halle • and with the Iustice speke;
On hem that ben gultyf • I wil ben awreke.
Lat non skape at the dore • take, ȝonge men, ȝeme;   825
For I wil be Iustice this day • domes for to deme.
God spede me this day • at my newe werk !
Adam, com on with me • for thou schalt be my clerk.'
His men answereden him • and bade him doon his best,
' And if thou to vs haue neede • thou schalt fynde vs prest; 830
We wiln stande with the • whil that we may dure,
And but we werke manly • pay vs non hure.'
'Yonge men,' seyde Gamelyn • 'so mot I wel the !
As trusty a maister • ȝe schal fynde of me.'
Right there as the Iustice • sat in the halle,   835
In wente Gamelyn • amonges hem alle.
  Gamelyn leet vnfetere • his brother out of bende.
Thanne seyde sire Ote • his brother that was hende,
' Thou haddest almost, Gamelyn • dwelled to longe,
For the quest is oute on me • that I schulde honge.'   840
' Brother,' seyde Gamelyn • 'so god ȝif me good rest !
This day they schuln ben hanged • that ben on thy quest;
And the Iustice bothe • that is the Iugge-man,
And the scherreue bothe • thurgh him it bigan.'
Thanne seyde Gamelyn • to the Iustise,   845

819. Cp. reed; Hl. red; *the rest* rede.   822. Hl. Pt. lat; *the
rest* late.   826. for *in* MS. Camb. Mm. 2. 5; *the rest omit.*
829. Rl. bade; *the rest* bad.   835. Rl. (17 D. xv) as; *which the
rest omit.*   837. Hl. beende; Cp. Pt. Ln. bende.   838. Hl.
Cp. heende; *the rest* hende.   843. Hl. *omits second* the. Hl. Iugges;
the rest Iugge, Iuge.   845. Cp. Thanne; *the rest* Than.

'Now is thy power y-don · thou most nedes arise;
Thow hast ȝeuen domes · that ben yuel dight,
I wil sitten in thy sete · and dressen hem aright.'
The Iustice sat stille · and roos nought anoon ;
And Gamelyn in haste · cleuede his cheeke-boon;   850
Gamelyn took him in his arm · and no more spak,
But threw him ouer the barre · and his arm to-brak.
Durste non to Gamelyn · seye but good,
For ferd of the company · that withoute stood.
Gamelyn sette him doun · in the Iustices seet,   855
And sire Ote his brother by him · and Adam at his feet.
Whan Gamelyn was i-set · in the Iustices stede,
Herkneth of a bourde · that Gamelyn dede.
He leet fetre the Iustice · and his false brother,
And dede hem come to the barre · that oon with that other. 860
Tho Gamelyn hadde thus y-doon · hadde he no rest,
Til he had enquered · who was on the quest
For to deme his brother · sir Ote, for to honge ;
Er he wiste which they were · him thoughte ful longe.
But as sone as Gamelyn · wiste wher they were,   865
He dede hem euerichone · feteren in-feere,
And bringen hem to the barre · and sette hem in rewe;
'By my faith !' seyde the Iustice · 'the scherreue is a schrewe!'
Than seyde Gamelyn · to the Iustise,
'Thou hast y-ȝeue domes · of the wors assise;   870
And the twelve sisours · that weren of the quest,
They schul ben hanged this day · so haue I good rest !'

850. Harl. (1758) in haste ; *which the rest omit.*   854. Rl. Harl.
(1758) ferd; Pt. feerd ; Hl. Cp. fered ; Ln. ferde.   855. MSS. sete.
857. Hl. Rl. Cp. sete (*for* stede, *wrongly*).   859. Cp. Ln. false ; *the
rest* fals.   861. Cp. hadde; Rl. hade; Hl. had (*2nd time*).   864.
Rl. Pt. him ; Harl. (1758) hym; Hl. Cp. Ln. he.   866. Cp.
feteren; Hl. fetere.   871. Rl. Pt. quest; Hl. Cp. Ln. queste.
872. Hl. *om.* good; *the rest have it.* Rl. Pt. rest ; Hl. Cp. Ln. reste.

Thanne seide the scherreue · to ȝonge Gamelyn,
'Lord, I crie the mercy · brother art thou myn.'
'Therfore,' seyde Gamelyn · 'haue thou Cristes curs,   875
For and thou were maister · ȝit I schulde haue wors.'
For to make short tale · and nouȝt to tarie longe,
He ordeyned him a quest · of his men so stronge;
The Iustice and the scherreue · bothe honged hye,
To weyuen with the ropes · and with the wynde drye;   880
And the twelue sisours · (sorwe haue that rekke!)
Alle they were hanged · faste by the nekke.
Thus ended the false knight · with his treccherie,
That euer had i-lad his lyf · in falsnes and folye.
He was hanged by the nekke · and nouȝt by the purs,   885
That was the meede that he hadde · for his fadres curs.

  Sire Ote was eldest · and Gamelyn was ȝing,
They wenten with here frendes · euen to the kyng;
They made pees with the kyng · of the best assise.
The kyng loued well sir Ote · and made him Iustise.   890
And after, the kyng made Gamelyn · bothe in est and west,
Chef Iustice · of al his fre forest;
Alle his wighte ȝonge men · the kyng forȝaf here gilt,
And sitthen in good office · the kyng hem hath i-pilt,
Thus wan Gamelyn · his lond and his leede,   895
And wrak him of his enemys · and quitte hem here meede;
And sire Ote his brother · made him his heir,
And siththen wedded Gamelyn · a wyf bothe good and feyr;

  877. Hl. tarie; *which the rest omit.*   878. Rl. Pt. Harl. (1758)
quest; *the rest* queste.   879. Cp. beþ; *the rest* bothe, both.   880.
Hl. *om.* the *before* ropes; *the rest have it.* Hl. Rl. Cp. wynd; *the rest*
wynde, winde.   883. Cp. Ln. false; *the rest* fals.   885. Hl. Pt. nek;
the rest necke, nekke.   886. Rl. Cp. hadde; *the rest* had.   888.
Hl. freendes. Hl. euen to; Rl. Harl. (1758) and passeden to; Pt. and
passed to; Cp. and passed with; Ln. and pesed with.   896. Cp. Pt.
quitte; Hl. quyt.

They lyueden to-gidere · whil that Crist wolde,
And sithen was Gamelyn · grauen vnder molde.   900
And so schal we alle · may ther no man fle :
God bringe vs to the Ioye · that euer schal be !

900. Hl. moolde.   902. Ln. bringe; *the rest* bryng, bring.

NOTES.

1. Litheth, hearken ye; cf. l. 169. This is the imperative plural; so also *lesteneth, herkeneth.* See remarks on the dialect in the Preface. For the explanation of the harder words, see the Glossary. Compare: 'Now list and *lithe,* you gentlemen'; Percy Folio MS., ii. 218; 'Now *lithe* and listen, gentlemen,' id. iii. 77.

3. Iohan of Boundys. It is not clear what is meant by *Boundys,* which is repeated in l. 226; nor is there any clear indication of the supposed locality of the story. Lodge, in his novel (see the Preface), ingeniously substitutes *Bourdeaux,* and calls the knight 'Sir John of Bourdeaux.'[1] In Shakespeare, he becomes Sir Roland de Bois.

The reading *righte* (for *right*) is demanded by grammar, the article being in the definite form; and the same reading is equally demanded by the metre. Where the final *e* is thus necessary to the grammar and metre alike, there is little difficulty in restoring the correct reading. Compare *the good-e knight* in ll. 11, 25, 33.

4. 'He was sufficiently instructed by right bringing up, and knew much about sport.' *Nurture* is the old phrase for 'a genteel education.' Thus we find 'The boke of *Nurture,* or Schoole of good maners: for men, seruants, and children,' written by Hugh Rhodes, and printed in 1577; and John Russell's 'Boke of Nurture,' in MS. Harl. 4011. See the Babees Book, ed. F. J. Furnivall, 1868; where much information as to the behaviour of our forefathers is given. By *game* is meant what is now called *sport*; 'The Master of the Game' is the name of an old treatise on hunting; see Reliquiæ Antiquæ, i. 149.

5. Thre sones, three sons. They are here named Johan, Ote, and Gamelyn; Lodge calls them Saladyne, Fernandine, and Rosader; in Shakespeare, they are Oliver, Jaques, and Orlando. The characters of the three are much the same in all three versions of the story.

6. Sone he began, he soon began, viz. to evince his disposition.

12. His day, his term of life, his lifetime. So in Hamlet, v. i. 315. the 'dog will have his *day*.' Hence *after his day* is, practically, after his death.

---

[1] The reading *Burdeuxs* actually occurs in MS. Camb. Univ. Lib. Ii. 3. 26. See *Boundys* in the Glossary; and see Pref. § 2.

14. 'This appears to mean, that the knight had himself acquired his land, and held it in fee simple (*verrey purchas*), not entailed nor settled; and that, consequently, he had a right to divide it among his children as he pleased. The *housbond* in this case means a man who was kept at home looking after his domestic business and his estates, and who could not be *wyde-wher*,' i.e. often far from home; note by Mr. Jephson. See ll. 58–61 below, which prove that the knight had partly inherited his land, and partly won it by military service. Cf. Chaucer, Prol. 256 (or 258), 319 (or 321). In the Freres Tale (C. T. 7031) we find:—

    'And here I ride about my *pourchasing*,
       To wote wher men wol giue me any-thing;
       My *pourchas* is theffect of all my rente.'

I cannot think that Dr. Morris is right in explaining *purchasyng* by 'prosecution'; see *Purchas* in the Glossary.

16. **Hadde**, might have; the subjunctive mood.

20. **On lyue**, in life; now written *a-live* or *alive*. *Lyue* is the dat. case, governed by *on*, which constantly has the sense of 'in' in A.S. and M.E.

23. **Ther**, where. The reader should note this common idiom, or he will miss the structure of the sentence. Cf. ll. 33, 52, 66, &c.

31. **Ne dismay you nought**, do not dismay yourself; i.e. be not dismayed or dispirited.

32. 'God can bring good out of the evil that is now wrought.' *Boot*, advantage, remedy, or profit, is continually contrasted with *bale* or evil; the alliteration of the words rendered them suitable for proverbial phrases. One of the commonest is 'When *bale* is hext, then *boot* is next,' i.e. when evil is highest (at its height), then the remedy is nighest. This is one of the Proverbs of Hendyng; see Specimens of English, ed. Morris and Skeat, part ii. p. 40. So, in l. 34, *Boote of bale* means 'remedy of evil,' good out of evil. See note to l. 631.

34. **It is no nay**, there is no denying it, it cannot be denied. So in Chaucer, C. T. 8692, 9015.

39. **That on, that other**, the one, the other. Sometimes corruptly written *the ton, the tother*; and hence the vulgar English *the tother*.

48. **Whan he good cowde**, when he knew what was good, i.e. when he was old enough to know right from wrong; or, as we now say, when he came to years of discretion. Observe that the division of land here proposed was not final; for the good knight, being still alive, altered it; see l. 54.

53. 'Saint Martin was a Hungarian by birth, and served in the army under Constantius and Julian. He is represented in pictures as a Roman knight on horseback, with his sword dividing his cloak into two pieces, one of which he gives to a beggar. He was a strenuous

opponent of the Arians, and died at Tours, where his relics were preserved and honoured.'—Jephson. St. Martin's day, commonly called Martinmas, is Nov. 11. The knight swears by St. Martin in his character of soldier. Cf. l. 225.

57. **Plowes**, ploughlands; see the Glossary.

62. The knight's intention was, evidently, that Gamelyn's share should be the best. In Lodge's novel, Sir John gives to the eldest 'fourteen ploughlands, with all my mannor-houses and my richest plate'; to the second, 'twelve ploughlands'; but to the youngest, says he, 'I give my horse, my armour, and my launce, with sixteene ploughlands; for, if the inwarde thoughts be discovered by outward shadows, Rosader wil exceed you all in bountie and honour.'

64. 'That my bequest may stand,' i.e. remain good.

67. **Stoon-stille**, as still as a stone. So Chaucer has 'as stille as stoon'; Clerkes Tale, l. 121. See ll. 263, 423.

76. 'And afterwards he paid for it in his fair skin.' We should now say, his recompense fell upon his own head.

78. **Of good wil**, readily, of their own accord. . 'They of their own accord feared him as being the strongest.' So also 'of thine own good will,' Shak. Rich. II. iv. 1. 177; 'by her good will,' Venus and Adonis, 479. But the nearest parallel passage is in Octouian Imperator, l. 561, pr. in Weber's Metrical Romances, iii. 180. It is there said of some sailors who were chased by a lioness, that they ran away very hastily 'with good wylle.' Cf. *in wille*, i.e. anxious, in l. 173.

82. To handle his beard, i.e. to feel, by his beard, that he was of full age. Lodge has a parallel passage. 'With that, casting up his hand, he felt haire on his face, and perceiving his beard to bud, for choler he began to blush, and swore to himselfe he would be no more subject to such slaverie.' Cf. As You Like It, iii. 2. 218, 396.

90. 'Is our meat prepared,' i.e. is our dinner ready? *Our* perhaps means *my*, being used in a lordly style. See the next note.

92. Observe the use of the familiar *thou*, in place of the usual respectful *ye*. This accounts for the elder brother's astonishment, as expressed in the next line.

100. 'Brother by name, and brother in that only.'

101. **That rape was of rees**, who was hasty in his fit of passion. Mr. Jephson's explanation 'deprived of reason for anger' is incorrect. *Rape* is hasty; see the Glossary. *Rees* is the modern E. *race*, A.S. *rǽs*, applied to any sudden course, whether bodily or mental; cf. l. 547. So in Gower, ed. Pauli, i. 335, we find :—

'Do thou no-thinge in suche a *rees*,'

i.e. do nothing in such a sudden fit; referring to Pyramus, who rashly slew himself upon the hasty false assumption that Thisbe was dead.

102. **Gadeling**, fellow; a term of reproach. But observe that the sarcasm lies in the similarity of the sound of the word to *Gamelyn*. Hence Gamelyn's indignant reply. In P. Plowman, C. xi. 297, *gade-lynges* are ranked with false folk, deceivers, and liars.

103. 'Thou shalt be glad to get mere food and clothing.'

109. **Ner**, nigher, the old *comparative* form; afterwards written *near*, and wrongly extended to *near-er*, with a *double* comparative suffix. Cf. l. 135, 352.

A.-foote, on foot; not *a foot*, the length of a foot, as that would have no final *e*.

115. **Schal algate**, must in any case.

116. This is obscure; it may mean 'unless *thou* art the one (to do it);' i. e. to give me the beating. In other words, Gamelyn dares his brother to use the rod himself, not to delegate such an office to another. But his brother was much too wary to take such advice; he preferred to depute the business to his men.

121. **Ouer-al**, all about, all round, everywhere.

122. **Stood**, i.e. which stood. The omission of the relative is common.

125. **Good woon**, good store; plentifully.

129. **For his eyȝe**, for awe of him. *His* is not the possessive pronoun here, but the genitive of the personal pronoun.

130. **By halues**, lit. by sides; i.e. some to one side, some to the other. *Drowe by halues* = sidled away.

131. 'May ye prosper ill!' Cf. Chaucer, Pard. Tale (Group C), l. 947.

136. 'I will teach thee some play with the buckler.' An allusion to the 'sword and buckler play,' described in Strutt, Sports and Pastimes, bk. iii. ch. 6. § 22. Not unlike our modern 'single-stick,' but with the addition of a buckler on the left arm. Strutt gives a picture from a Bodleian MS., dated 1344, in which clubs or bludgeons are substituted for swords; and, no doubt, the swords used in sport were commonly of wood. Gamelyn is speaking jocosely; he had no buckler, but he had a wooden 'pestel,' which did very well for a sword.

137. 'By Saint Richard was a favourite oath[1] with the outlaws of Robin Hood's stamp, probably because of his Saxon extraction'; Jephson. Mr. Jephson adds the following quotation from the English Martyrologe, 1608. 'Saint Richard, King and Confessor, was sonne to Lotharius, King of Kent, who, for the love of Christ, taking upon him a long peregrination, went to Rome for devotion to that sea [*see*], and, on his way homeward, died at Lucca, about the year of Christ 750, where his body is kept until this day, with great veneration, in the

---

[1] No quotation is given to support this assertion.

oratory and chappell of St. Frigidian, and adorned with an epitaph both in verse and prose.' But this is altogether beside the mark ; for Mr. Jephson certainly refers to the wrong saint. There were four St. Richards, commemorated, respectively, on Feb. 7, April 3, June 9, and August 21 ; see Alban Butler's Lives of the Saints. The day of the Saxon king is Feb. 7 ; but he could hardly have been so fresh in the memory of Englishmen as the more noted St. Richard, bishop of Chichester, who died in 1253, and was canonised in 1262 ; his day being April 3. There is a special fitness in the allusion to this latter saint, because he was a pattern of *brotherly love*, and Johan is here deprecating Gamelyn's anger. Alban Butler says of him : ' The un-fortunate situation of his eldest brother's affairs gave him an occasion of exercising his benevolent disposition. Richard condescended to become his *brother's servant*, undertook the management of his farms, and by his industry and generosity effectually retrieved his brother's before distressed circumstances.' His name still appears in our Prayer-books.

154. 'And mind that thou blame me, unless I soon grant it.'

156. 'If we are to be at one,' i. e. to be reconciled. Cf. l. 166.

158. 'Thou must cause me to possess it, if we are not to quarrel.'

160. We should now say—'All that your father left you, and more too, if you would like to have it.' The offer is meant to be very liberal.

164. 'As he well knew (how to do).'

167. 'In no respect he knew with what sort of a false treason his brother kissed him.' *Whiche* is cognate with the Latin *qualis*, and has here the same sense.

171. 'There was a wrestling-match proclaimed there, hard by.'

172. 'And, as prizes for it, there were exhibited a ram and a ring.' In Lodge's novel, 'a day of wrestling and tournament' is appointed by Torimond, king of France. In Chaucer's Prologue, l. 548 (*or* 550) we find : 'At wrastling he wolde bere awey the ram.' On this Tyrwhitt has the following note : ' This was the usual prize at wrestling-matches. See C. T. l. 13671 [Sir Thopas, st. 5], and Gamelyn, ll. 184, 280. Matthew Paris mentions a wrestling-match at Westminster, A.D. 1222, at which a ram was the prize.' In Strutt's Sports and Pastimes, bk. ii, ch. 2, § 14, two men are represented as wrestling for a live cock. Strutt also quotes a passage from ' A mery Geste of Robin Hode,' which gives an account of a wrestling, at which the following prizes were ' set up ' (the same phrase being used as here), viz. a white bull, a courser with saddle and bridle, a pair of gloves, a *red gold ring*, and a pipe of wine !

199. 'Why dost thou thus behave?' i. e. make this lamentation. Cf. As You Like It, i. 2. 133-140.

204. 'Unless God be surety for them,' i. e. ensure their recovery,

The story supposes that the two sons are not slain, but greatly disabled; as Shakespeare says, 'there is little hope of life' in them.

206. **With the nones,** on the occasion that, provided that. *For the nones,* for the occasion, stands for *for then ones,* for the once ; so here *with the nones = with then ones,* with the once. *Then* is the dat. case of the article, being a weakened form of A.S. *ðám.* Cf. l. 456.

207. **Wilt thow wel doon,** if thou wishest to do a kind deed.

214. **Drede not of,** fear not for.

217. 'How he dared adventure himself, to prove his strength upon him that was so doughty a champion?'

224. **Whil he oouthe go,** whilst he was able to go about.

230. **A moohe schrewe thou were,** thou wast a great doer of mischief. Gamelyn retorts that he is now *a more,* i.e. a still greater doer of mischief. *Moche* is often used of size. In Havelok, l. 982, *more than the meste =* bigger than the biggest.

236. **Gonne goon,** did go. *Gonne* is a mere auxiliary verb.

237. 'The champion tried various sleights upon Gamelyn, who was prepared for them.'

240. **Fast aboute,** busily employed, trying your best. Cf. l. 785.

248. Spoken ironically, 'shall it be counted as a throw, or as none?'

249. **Whether, &c.,** whichever it be accounted.

253. **Of him, &c.,** he stood in no awe of him. Instead of our modern expression 'he stood in awe of him,' the M. E. expression is, usually, 'he stood awe of him,' suppressing *in.* It probably arose out of the very construction here used, viz. 'awe of him stood to him,' i.e. arose in him. However that may be, the idiom is common. Thus, in Barbour's Bruce, iii. 62 :—

> 'Quhen that the lord of Lorne saw
> His men stand off him ane sik awe.'

In Havelok, l. 277 :—

> 'Al Engelond of him stod awe,
> Al Engelond was of him adrad.'

So also : 'he stode of him non eye'; Rob. of Brunne, tr. of Langtoft, p. 8, l. 24. So also in Wallace, v. 929, vi. 878.

255. 'Who was not at all well pleased.'

256. 'He is master of us all.'

257. 'It is full yore ago'; it is very long ago.

262. **Wil nomore,** desires no more, has had enough.

270. 'This fair is done.' A proverb, meaning that the things of the fair are all sold, and there is no more business to be done.

271. 'As I hope to do well, I have not yet sold up the half of my ware'; i.e. I have more to offer. The wrestler, in spite of his pain, utters the grim joke that Gamelyn sells his ware too dearly.

244 compare Owl and Nightingale. "ore maistrie."

272. *Haluendel* is for A.S. *healfne dæl* or *þone healfan dæl*, the accusative case. The word *of* is to be understood after it. See Zupitza's Notes to Guy of Warwick.

273. See note to l. 334.

276. **Lakkest**, dispraisest, decriest. In P. Plowman, B. v. 130, we find 'to blame mennes ware'; and, only two lines below, the equivalent phrase 'to lakke his chaffare.'

277. 'By Saint James in Galicia.' In Chaucer's Prologue, the Wife of Bath had been 'in Galice at Seint Jame.' The shrine of St. James, at Compostella in Galicia, was much frequented by pilgrims. See my note to P. Plowman, B. prol. 47. It is remarkable that *the whole of this line* is quoted from A Poem on the Times of Edw. II., l. 475; see Political Songs, ed. Wright, p. 345. It occurs again below, l. 764.

278. 'Yet it is too cheap, that which thou hast bought.' The franklin tells the defeated wrestler that it is not for him to call Gamelyn's ware dear, for he has, in fact, been let off much too cheaply. Our modern *cheap* is short for *good cheap*, i.e. bought in good market. *To buy in a good cheap* was shortened to *to buy good cheap*, and finally became *to buy cheap*.

281. **Haue**, have, receive, take.

285. **Rowte**, company. We are to suppose that a crowd of Gamelyn's admirers accompanied him home. In Lodge's novel, the elder brother 'sawe wher Rosader returned with the garland on his head, as having won the prize, accompanied with a crue of boon companions; greeved at this, he stepped in and shut the gate.'

297. See note to l. 334.

302. **Though thou haddest swore**, though thou hadst sworn (the contrary). This curious phrase occurs also in Chaucer, Kn. Tale, l. 231, where 'although we hadde it sworn' is equivalent to 'though we had sworn (the contrary).'

312. 'That desired either to walk or to ride in.' *Go*, when opposed to *ride*, means to go on foot, to walk.

318. **And ȝe wil doon after me**, if ye will act according to my advice; spoken parenthetically.

321. **Oure catour**, caterer for us. **Oure aller purs**, the purse of us all. Cf. l. 256.

324. **Largely**, liberally; the usual old meaning.

328. **No cheste**, no strife, no quarrelling.

334. **So**, &c., 'as I hope to enjoy the use of my eye'; lit. 'as I may use my eye.' This phrase occurs also in Havelok, 2545 : 'So mote ich brouke mi rith eie,' as I hope to have the use of my right eye. And again in the same, l. 1743, with the substitution of 'finger or toe' for 'right eye'; and in l. 311, with the substitution of 'mi blake swire,' i. e.

my black neck ; cf. ll. 273, 297 above. See also ll. 407, 489, 567. Even
Chaucer has : 'So mot I brouke wel myn eyen twaye,' as I hope to make
good use of my two eyes ; Nonne Prestes Tale, 479.

338. **Bitaughte** is used in two senses ; they commended Gamelyn to
God's protection, and bade him good day.

345. **Mangerye**, feast, lit. an eating. It occurs in P. Plowman,
C. xiii. 46 ; Wyclif, Works, ed. Arnold, i. 4. In Sir Amadace, st. 55, a
wedding-feast is called a *maungery*, and lasted 40 days ; Early Eng.
Metrical Romances, ed. Robson, p. 49. Cf. ll. 434, 464.

352. **Ful neer**, much nearer. See note to l. 109.

366. *Iohan* was pronounced like mod. E. Joan, and rimes with *noon*,
pronounced as *noan*. So also in Chaucer, Man of Lawes Tale, l. 1019.

367. 'By my faith' ; cf. l. 555. Chaucer has 'by my fey' ; Kn. Tale,
268.

368. 'If thou thinkest the same as thou sayst, may God requite it
thee !'

372. **Tho**, when. **Threwe**, didst throw ; observe the absence of *-st*
in the suffix of the second person of the past tense of strong verbs.

373. **Moot**, meeting, assembly, concourse of people ; in allusion to
the crew of companions whom Gamelyn introduced. Moreover, the
word *moot* was especially used of an assembly of men in council, like
our modern *meeting*. But it is, perhaps, simpler to take it in the sense
of hostile meeting, dispute, strife ; cf. St. Katharine, l. 1314, and cf.
M. E. *motien*, to dispute. Indeed, as the rimes are often imperfect, the
original word may have been *mood*, i. e. anger.

376. It was not uncommon, to prevent a person from being forsworn,
that the terms of an oath should be literally fulfilled ; cf. Merch. Ven. iv.
1. 326. In his novel, Lodge avoids all improbability by a much simpler
device. He makes the eldest brother surprise the youngest in his sleep.
'On a morning very early he cald up certain of his servants, and went
with them to the chamber of Rosader, which being open, he entered with
his crue, and surprized his brother when he was asleepe, and bound him
with fetters,' &c.

382. Here, as in l. 420, all the MSS. have *honde*. The final *e* probably represents the dative or *instrumental* case, and the correct reading
is *fote and honde*, as in MSS. Pt. and Ln. in both passages.

386. **Wood**, mad. It was common to bind and starve madmen, and
to treat them cruelly. Even Malvolio was to be put 'in a dark room
and bound' ; Tw. Nt. iii. 4. 147. Cf. As You Like It, iii. 2. 421.

394. **Or**, ere, before ; not 'or.' **Be**, been.

398. '*Spence*, or (according to the original French form of the
word) *despense*, was the closet or room in convents and large houses
where the victuals, wine, and plate were locked up ; and the person who

had the charge of it was called the *spencer*, or the *despencer*. Hence originated two common family names.'—Wright. The *spence*, however, like the *spencer*, owed its name to the O.F. verb *despendre*, to spend; as explained in my Etym. Dict., s.v. *Spend*. See the Glossary. Lodge retains the name of Adam Spencer; whence Adam in Shakespeare.

411. 'Upon such an agreement.'

413. 'All as I may prosper'; as I hope to thrive.

414. 'I will hold covenant with thee, if thou wilt loose me.'

430. Wher I go, whether shall I go. *Wher* is a contracted form of *whether*, like *or* for *other*. Girde of, strike off.

433. That this, &c., that this is a thing not to be denied, a sure thing.

438. Hem, them, i. e. the fetters (understood); cf. l. 498.

441. Borwe the, be surety for thee, go bail for thee.

444. Do an other, act in another way, try another course. There is no authority for inserting *thing* after *other*.

445. Lodge says: 'and at the ende of the hall shall you see stand a couple of good pollaxes, one for you and another for me.'

449. 'If we must in any case absolve them of their sin.' Said jocosely; he was going to absolve them after a good chastisement.

451. St. Charity was the daughter of St. Sophia, who christened her three daughters *Fides*, *Spes*, and *Caritas*; see Butler's Lives of the Saints (Aug. 1).

453. Lodge says: 'When I give you a wincke,' &c.

456. For the nones, for the occasion; see note to l. 206.

460. Leste and meste, least and greatest.

461. Halle, of the hall; A. S. *healle*, gen. case of *heal*, a hall. In l. 496, we may take *halle-dore* as a compound word, but *halle* is still a genitive form.

471. Ther that, where that; as commonly.

481. 'Who beggeth for thee (to come) out of prison, or who may be surety for thee; but ever may it be well with them that cause thee much sorrow.'

485. 'All that may be surety for thee, may evil befal them.'

489. So, &c., 'as I hope to make use of my bones,' lit. bone.

503. 'Gamelyn sprinkles holy water with an oaken sprig.' Said jocosely; Gamelyn flourishes his staff like one who sprinkles holy water. A *spire* is properly a springing shoot, hence a sprig or sapling. See the Glossary.

509. Mr. Jephson here remarks as follows:—'The hatred of church-men, of holy water, and of everything connected with the church, observable in all the ballads of this class, is probably owing to the fact, that William the Conqueror and his immediate successors systematically removed the Saxon bishops and abbots, and intruded Normans in their

stead into all the valuable preferments in England.　But there were also other grounds for the odium in which these foreign prelates were held. Sharing in the duties of the common law judges, they participated in the aversion with which the functionaries of the law were naturally regarded by outlaws and robbers,' &c.　He also quotes, from the Lytel Geste of Robin Hood, the following :

> ' These bysshopes and these archebysshoppes,
> 　　Ye shall them beete and bynde ;
> The high sheryfe of Notynghame,
> 　　Hym holde ye in your mynde.'

It may be added that Lodge entirely omits here all mention of abbot, prior, monk, or canon.　Times had changed.

514. ' Pay a liberal allowance,' i. e. deal your blows bountifully.

So euer, &c., ' as sure as ever I hear mass.'　Cf. l. 595.

520. **Telle largely**, count fully.

523. **The croune**, i. e. the crown of each man's head ; alluding to the tonsure.　It means, do not spoil the tonsure on their crowns, but break their legs and arms.

531. **Cold reed**, cold counsel, unprofitable counsel.　So in Chaucer, Nonne Prestes Tale, 435, 436, we find : ' Wommennes counseils ben ful ofte *colde*; Wommannes counseil broughte us first *to woo*.'　Storm notes the same idiom in Icelandic, *köld eru opt kvenna-råð*, women's counsels are oft-times fatal ; see *kaldr* in the Icel. Dict.　So Shakespeare has '*colder* tidings'; Rich. III, iv. 4. 536.　Cf. l. 759 below.

532. ' It had been better for us.'　Cf. l. 621.

533. This is ironical, and refers, as Mr. Jephson rightly says, to the *laying on of hands*, whereby Gamelyn made his victims deacons and priests after a new fashion of his own.

543. **Here loue**, love of them ; **here awe**, awe of them.　*Here* = A.S. *hira*, gen. pl. of *hé*, he.　Hence *here* means 'their,' as in l. 569.

558. **Ther . . inne**, wherein (Gamelyn was).

567. ' As I hope to have the use of my chin.'　See note to l. 334.

578. ' I will repay thee for thy words, when I see my opportunity.'

583. **It ben**, they are ; lit. it are.　A common idiom in Middle English.　See P. Plowman, C. vi. 59, ix. 217, xvi. 309 ; and compare *it am I*, as in Chaucer, Man of Lawes Tale, l. 1109.

588. ' Make their beds in the fen,' i. e. lie down in the fen or mud.

596. Spoken ironically.　Adam offers them some refreshment.　They reply, that his wine is not good, being too strong ; indeed, so strong that it will not only, like ordinary wine, steal away a man's brains, but even take them out of his head altogether, so that they lie scattered in his hood.　In other words, Adam's staff breaks their heads, and lets the brains out.

606. 'It is better for us to be there at large.'

609. Lodge says that they 'tooke their way towards the forest of Arden.'

610. 'Then the sheriff found the nest, but no egg (in it).' So also in William of Palerne, l. 83 : 'Than fond he nest and no neiȝ · for nouȝt nas ther leued'; i. e. for nothing was left there. *No neiȝ = non eiȝ*, no egg.

616. **And loke how he fare,** and let us see how he may fare.

618. Here Adam merely expresses disgust of his new mode of life. In Lodge's novel, he begins to faint, being old. Cf. l. 817.

621. **Leuer me were,** it would be preferable for me.

631. 'After misery comes help.' So in the Proverbs of Hendyng, as said above, in note to l. 32. Trench, in his book On Proverbs, quotes a Hebrew proverb :—When the tale of bricks is doubled, Moses comes.

642. 'Whoso looked aright,' i. e. if one were to look carefully.

651. I. e. I only curse (or blame) myself if I yield.

652. 'Though ye fetched five more, ye would then be only twelve in number.' He means that he would fight twelve of them.

660. In Lodge's novel, the chief is 'Gerismond the lawfull King of France, banished by Torismond, who with a lustie crue of Outlawes lived in that Forrest.' But the present text evidently refers to an English outlaw, such as Robin Hood.

666. 'I will adventure myself as far as the door.' Spoken proverbially, there being no door in the wood. He means that he will venture within sight of the chief. **Hadde mete,** might have food.

689. 'His peace was made'; i. e. his pardon had been obtained.

698. 'And caused his brother to be indicted.'

700. **Wolues-heed,** wolf's head. 'This was the ancient Saxon formula of outlawry, and seems to have been literally equivalent to setting the man's head at the same estimate as a wolf's head. In the laws of Edward the Confessor [§ 6], it is said of a person who has fled justice, 'Si postea repertus fuerit et teneri possit, vivus regi reddatur, vel caput ipsius si se defenderit; lupinum enim caput geret a die utlagacionis sue, quod ab Anglis *wluesheued* nominatur. Et hec sententia communis est de omnibus utlagis.'—Wright. See Thorpe, Ancient Laws, &c., i. 445.

701. **Of his men,** i. e. (some) of his men.

703. 'How the wind was turned'; i. e. which way the wind blew, as we now say.

704. 'When a man's lands were seized by force or unjustly, the peasantry on the estates were exposed to be plundered and ill-treated by the followers of the intruder.'—Wright.

707. 'The messengers of ill tidings, however innocent themselves, often experienced all the first anger of the person to whom they carried

them, in the ages of feudal power. Hence the bearer of ill news generally began by deprecating the wrath of the person addressed.'— Wright. This was not, however, peculiar to those times. Cf. Sophocles, Antigone, 228; 2 Hen. IV. i. 1. 100; Rich. III. iv. 4. 510; Macb. v. 5. 39.

709. 'I. e. has obtained government of the bailiwick. In former times .. the high sheriff was the officer personally responsible for the peace of his bailiwick, which he maintained by calling out the *posse comitatus* to assist him.'—Jephson.

710. Doth the orie, causes thee to be proclaimed.

713. 'Greet well my husbands (i. e. servants) and their wives.' The A.S. *wif* was a neuter substantive, and remained unchanged in the plural, like *sheep* and *deer* in modern English. We find *wif* as a pl. form also in Layamon, l. 1507. The present is a very late example.

714. 'I will (soon) be in the next shire,' i. e. I will soon come to the adjoining county. This expression shows that the author is really laying the scene in England. In venturing into the shire of which his brother was sheriff, Gamelyn was boldly putting himself into his brother's power.

718. 'Put down his hood,' lowered his hood, so as to show his face.

724. Leet take Gamelyn, caused (men) to take Gamelyn; we now say 'caused Gamelyn to be taken,' changing the verb from active to passive. The active use of the verb is universal in such phrases in Middle English, and is still common in German. 'Er liess Gamelyn nehmen.' Cf. l. 733.

727. Ote is not a common name; we find mention of 'Sir Otes de Lile' in Libius Disconius, l. 1103, in the Percy Folio MS., ii. 455.

732. Wonder sory, wonderfully sorry. Nothing light, in no degree light-hearted.

738. 'May evil befall such another brother (as thou art).'

744. 'I offer to bail him,' lit. I bid for him for bail; *mainprise* being a sb., and *him* a dative case. Mr. Jephson says—'I demand that he be granted to me on mainprise, or bail, till the assize for general gaol-delivery.'

752. 'Cause (men) to deliver him at once, and to hand him over to me.'

761. Sit, sits; short for sitteth. Such contractions are common in the 3rd pers. sing. of the pres. indicative. So also *stant* = standeth, &c. See note to l. 806. In l. 749, *sitte* means 'may sit.'

779. Cors, curse. He was never cursed by those with whom he had dealings. This can only refer to the poor whom he never oppressed. The author quietly ignores the strong language of the churchmen whom he stripped of everything. This is precisely the tone adopted in the Robin Hood ballads.

785. **Fast aboute,** busily employed. See l. 240.

786. **To hyre the quest,** to suborn the jury. See l. 801.

790. **Seet,** should sit. The A.S. for *sat* is *sæt*, but for *should sit* (3rd pers. sing. of the pt. t. subj.) is *sǽte*. The latter became the M.E. *seete*; hence *seet*, by loss of the final *e*. It rimes with *beheet* (A.S. *behét*).

806. **Spet,** short for *speedeth*; see note to l. 761.

834. **Of,** in. So in Shakespeare, Jul. Cæsar, ii. i. 157—'We shall find *of* him A shrewd contriver.'

840. **The quest is oute,** the verdict is (already) delivered.

852. **The barre,** the bar in front of the justice's seat; see ll. 860, 867.

864. 'It seemed a very long time to him.'

871. **Sisours,** jury-men. I copy the following from my note on P. Plowman, B. 2. 62. 'The exact signification of *sisour* does not seem quite certain, and perhaps it has not always the same meaning. The Low-Latin name was *assissores* or *assissiarii*, interpreted by Ducange to mean 'qui a principe vel a domino feudi delegati *assisias* tenent'; whence Halliwell's explanation of *sisour* as a person deputed to hold assizes. Compare—

> 'Þys fals men, þat beyn *sysours*,
> þat for hate a trew man wyl endyte,
> And a þefe for syluer quyte.'
>
> Robert of Brunne, Handlyng Synne, 1335.

Mr. Furnivall's note says—'*Sysour*, an inquest-man at assizes. The *sisour* was really a juror, though differing greatly in functions and in position from what jurymen subsequently became; see Forsyth's Hist. of Trial by Jury.' In the tale of Gamelyn, however, it is pretty clear that 'the twelve sisours that weren of the quest' were simply the twelve gentlemen of the jury, who were hired to give false judgment (l. 786).' Blount, in his Law Dictionary, says of *assisors*, that 'in Scotland (according to Skene) they are the same with our jurors.' The following stanza from A Poem on the Times of Edw. II., ll. 469–474 (printed in Political Songs, ed. Wright, p. 344) throws some light on the text:—

> 'And thise *assisours*, that comen to shire and to hundred,
> Damneth men for silver, and that nis no wonder.
> For whan the riche justise wol do wrong for mede,
> Thanne thinketh hem thei muwen the bet, for thei han more nede
>   to winne.
> Ac so is al this world ablent, that no man douteth sinne.'

880. 'To swing about with the ropes, and to be dried in the wind.'

881. 'Sorrow may he have who cares for it.' Not an uncommon phrase. In P. Plowman, B. vi. 122, it appears as 'þe deuel haue þat reccheth,' i. e. take him who regrets it.

885. This seems to mean, ' he was hanged by the neck, and not by the purse.' That is, he was really hanged, and not merely made to suffer in his purse by paying a fine; cf. Ch. Prol. 657.

889. **Of the best assise**, in the truest manner; cf. l. 544.

900. ' Buried under the earth.'

901. ' No man can escape it.'

GLOSSARIAL INDEX.

The usual contractions occur, such as A. S. = Anglo-Saxon; M. E. = Middle English; F. = French; Icel. = Icelandic (Cleasby and Vigfusson); O. F. = Old French; Prompt. Parv. = Promptorium Parvulorum, ed. Way (Camden Society). For the etymology of words that are still in use, the reader is referred to my Etymological Dictionary, or to the abridgment of it entitled 'A Concise Etymological Dictionary of the English Language.'

The following abbreviations are employed in a special sense : *v.* = verb in the infinitive mood; *pr. s.* or *pt. s.* means the *third* person singular of the present or past tense indicative, except when 1 or 2 (for *first* person or *second* person) is prefixed; similarly, *pr. pl.* or *pt. pl.* refers to the *third* person plural of the same tenses; *imp. s.* means the *second* person singular of the imperative mood. The references are to the lines of the Poem.

A fyue myle, a (space of) five miles, 545.

Abegge, *v.* pay for, 816. A. S. *ábycgan,* to buy, pay for. Hence Tudor-E. *abide,* by mistake for *aby.* See **Aboughte.**

Abide, *pp.* dwelt, remained, 337. The *i* is short. A. S. *ábiden,* pp. of *ábídan.* See **Abyde.**

Aboughte, *pt. s.* paid (for it), 76. See **Abegge.**

Aboute, *in phr.* fast aboute, i. e. very eager, busily employed, 240, 785.

Abyde, *ger.* to await, 24.

Adam, 398, 399, 403, &c.

A-dight, *pp.* treated, 731; accoutred, 628, 641. From A. S. *á-,* intensive prefix; and *dihtan,* to arrange, borrowed from Lat. *dictare.*

Adoun, *adv.* down, 149, 679.

Adrad, *pp.* afraid, 562. Pp. of *adreden,* to fear greatly; A. S. *ofdrǽdan.*

Afore, *prep.* before, 656.

Aforn, *adv.* before, in front, 806.

After, *prep.* according to, 56; Aftir, 819; After me, according to my counsel, 318; Sente after, sent for, 17.

Agast, *pp.* afraid (in a good sense), 7; afraid, terrified, 128, 152, 287, 383, 526, 810.

Algate, *adv.* in any case, by all means, 115, 449.

Aller, of all; Our aller, of us all, 321. See **Alther.** A. S. *ealra,* gen. pl. of *eal,* all.

Allowe, *v.* approve, make good, recompense, 578. O. F. *allouer,* from Lat. *allaudare.*

Almight, *adj.* almighty, 631. A.S. *ælmiht.*

E

Alonged, *pp.* filled with longing, 636. From the pp. of A. S. *of-langian,* to long after.

Al-so, *adv.* just as, as, 227; as, 379.

Alther, *gen. pl. adj.* of all; Our alther, of us all, 256. A later form of **Aller,** which see.

Altogidere, *adv.* wholly, 730.

Amonges, *prep.* amongst, 836.

Amys, *adv.* amiss, wrongly. 37.

And, *conj.* if, 156, 318, 368, 414, 797, 819, 876. Often shortened to *an,* esp. in later times; but really identical with the usual copulative conjunction.

Anon, *adv.* immediately, at once, 69, 115, 117; Anoon, 219, 849. A. S. *on án,* lit. in one (moment).

Anon-right, *adv.* straightway, 734.

Ar, *adv.* ere, before this, till now, 96; Ar that, ere that, 605. A. S. *ér.*

Aright, *adv.* rightly, 1, 29, 642.

Ariseth, *imp. pl.* arise ye, 643.

Armure, *s.* armour, 98.

Arst, *adv.* erst, formerly, before, 538. A. S. *érest,* superl. of *ér;* see **Ar.**

Aspyed, *pp.* espied. 490.

Assise, *s.* assize, 870, 889.

Assoile, *v.* absolve, 449; Assoyled, *pp.* 516.

Atte (*for* at the), at the, 136, 464; Atte gate, at the gate, 575; Atte laste, at the last, finally, 408; Atte mete, at meat, 629.

A-twynne, *adv.* asunder, 317.

Auauncement, *s.* advancement, promotion, 418.

Auentures, *s. pl.* adventures, 777.

Auntre, *v.* adventure myself, 666; Auntre him, adventure himself, 217. Short for *aventure,* old form of *adventure.*

Auow, *s.* vow, 378. Not an uncommon form; used by Chaucer.

Awe, *s.* awe, fear, 543.

Awreke, *pp.* avenged, 723, 824. A. S. *áwrecen,* pp. of *á-wrecan,* to avenge.

Ay, *s.* egg, 610. See the note. A. S. *æg.* ' It was not worthe an ay'; Rob. of Brunne, tr. of Langtoft, p. 181, l. 8.

Aȝein, *adv.* again, 771; Aȝen, back again, 528.

Aȝein, *prep.* against, 548. A. S. *ongéan.*

B.

Baillye, *s.* bailiwick, power of a bailiff, 709. ' *Baillie,* seigneury, government, authority; ... also a bailiwick, or country [i. e. county] justiceship'; Cotgrave.

Bale, *s.* mischief, evil, 32, 34. 631. A. S. *bealu.*

Barre, *s.* bar (of justice), 852, 867.

Be, 2 *pr. pl. as fut.* will be, 652; 2 *pr. s. subj.* mayest be, 116.

Beheet, *pt. s.* promised, 788. A. S. *behét,* pt. t. of *be-hátan,* to promise. See **Biheet.**

Bende, *s.* bond, captivity, 837; Bendes, *pl.* bonds, fetters, 457. A. S. *bend,* a bond.

Berde, *s.* beard, 82.

Bet, *adv.* better, 112.

Beten, *pp.* beaten, 115; Beteth, *imp. pl.* beat ye. 111.

Bi-falle, *pp.* happened, 685.

Biheet, 1 *pt. s.* promised, 378; *pt. s.* 418. A. S. *behét,* pt. t. of *be-hátan.* See **Beheet.**

Bileued, *pp.* left, 98; cf. l. 86.

Biquath, 360. See **Byquethe.**

Bisyde, *prep.* beside, 181.

Bitaughte, *pt. s.* commended, 338. See the note.

Blyue, *adv.* quickly, 19, 585. Short for *by lyue,* i. e. with life, in a lively way.

Bokeler, *s.* buckler, 136. See the note.

Bon, *s.* bone, 489. See **Boones.**

Bond, *pt. s.* bound. 818.

Bonde-men, *pl.* husbandmen, labourers. 699. The prefix has no connection with the verb to *bind,*

but is the same as Icel. *búandi,*
bóndi, a tiller of the soil.

Boone, *s.* boon, 153 ; Bone, 149.

Boones, *pl.* bones, 142. See Bon.

Boote, 34, 631. See Bote.

Bore, *pp.* born, 201, 252. Short
for A. S. *boren.*

Borwe, *s.* pledge, bail, 795. A. S.
borh, borg.

Borwe, *v.* go bail for, 441 ; *pr. pl.
subj.* 485 ; *pr. s; subj.* preserve,
save, 204. A. S. *borgian.*

Bote, *s.* remedy, help, good, 32 ;
Boote, 34, 631. A. S. *bót.*

Bothen, both, 625.

Boundys, a place-name ; perhaps
bounds, marches, border-land ; or
possibly Bons, near Falaise in Normandy. The Camb. MS. Ii. 3. 26
has *Burdeuxs,* Bordeaux. See l. 3.

Bour, *s.* bower, apartment, 405.
A. S. *búr.*

Bourde, *s.* jest, 858. ‘ *Bourde,* a
jeast, fib, tale of a tub ’ ; Cotgrave.

Broke-bak, broken-backed, 720.

Brother, *gen.* brother’s, 316.

Brouke, 1 *pr. s. subj.* may have the
use of, as (I) hope to continue to
use, 273, 334, 407, 489, 567 ;
Browke, 297. See note to l. 334.
A. S. *brúcan,* to use, enjoy.

But, *conj.* unless, 154.

But-if, *conj.* unless, 204, 749.

By, *prep.* during, 65.

Byforn, *adv.* beforehand, 452.

Bygan, *pt. s.* began (to show it), 6 ;
began, 82.

Byleued, *pp.* left, 86. See Bileued.

Bylynne, *v.* tarry, 557. A. S.
blinnan, short for *belinnan,* to
cease ; from A. S. *linnan,* to be
deprived of.

Byquethe, 1 *pr. s.* bequeath, 62 ;
Byquath, *pt. s.* 99, 157, 160.

Byreued, *pp.* stolen, 85, 97. E.
bereave.

Byseke, 1 *pr. s.* beseech, 35, 63.

Bysiden, *adv.* close by, 171 ; Her
bisyde, close by here, 178.

Byspak, *pt. s.* spake, addressed
(him), 101.

By-stad, *pp.* bestead, circumstanced,
676.

Bystrood, *pt. s.* bestrode, 189.

C.

Cam, *pt. s.* came, 282, 285.

Care, *s.* grief, sorrow, trouble, 200,
275, 615.

Cared, *pt. s.* was anxious, thought
anxiously, 11.

Cark, *s.* charge, responsibility, 760.
Anglo-F. *cark,* the same word as
F. *charge,* a load, charge.

Cart-staf, cart-staff, 590. (Perhaps
a staff to support the shafts of a
cart).

Cast, *s.* throw, 248.

Caste, *pt. s.* cast ; Caste tornes, tried
tricks, 237.

Catour, *s.* caterer, provider, 321.
Short for *acatour;* from Anglo-F.
acate, atat, the same as F. *ackat,*
a buying, purchase.

Champioun, *s.* champion, 203, 218,
219, 223, 227, &c.

Chanoun, *s.* canon, 599, 781.

Charite, *s.* charity, love ; For seinte
charite, for the sake of St. Charity,
513 ; also used with *bi,* 451. Cf.
Chaucer, Kn. Tale, 863. Ophelia
also says *by Saint Charity* ; Haml.
iv. 5. 58. (There was such a
saint ; see note.)

Cheep, *s.* market ; To good cheep,
too cheaply, lit. ‘ in too good a
market,’ 278.

Cheere, *s.* face ; Foul cheere, dis-
pleased look, 319 ; Foul chere,
534.

Chese, *imp. s.* choose, 180. A. S.
céosan.

Cheste, *s.* quarrelling, dispute, 328.
A. S. *céast,* strife, dispute, con-
tention.

Clepeth, *pr. s.* calls, 106 ; Clepide,
pt. s. 110. A. S. *cleopian.*

Cleuede, *pt. s.* cleft, 850. The

A. S. *cléofan,* to cleave, is properly a strong verb, with pt. t. *cléaf.*

Cold, *adj.* evil, discouraging, 531, 759.

Colen, *ger.* to cool, 540.

Come, 2 *pt. s.* hast come, 222; Com, *pt. s.* came, 68; Come, 1 *pr. s. subj.* may come, 795; Comen, *pt. pl.* came, 23, 386, 388; Comen, *pp.* 10, 291.

Compas, *adv.* in a circle, 629. A similar use of *compas* for *in compas* occurs in the Cursor Mundi, 2275 —'Ten myle *compas* al aboute.'

Conne, 2 *pr. pl.* know, 63.

Contek, *s.* strife, quarrel, 132. O.F. *contek,* strife.

Continaunce, *s.* demeanour, 262.

Cors, *s.* curse, 779. See Curs.

Counseil, *s.* counsel, 42.

Couthe, *pt. s.* knew (how), 164; could, 466; Cowthe, knew, 244; Cowthe, could, 174; Cowde, knew, 4, 48 (see note). A. S. *cúðe,* pt. t. of *cunnan.*

Croune, *s.* the clerical tonsure, 523.

Cryed, *pp.* proclaimed, 171, 183, 700.

Curs, *s.* curse, 8, 100. A. S. *curs.*

D.

Dalte, *pt. s.* divided, 65; Dalten, *pt. pl.* 45. See Delen.

Day, *s.* life-time, 12, 65.

Dede, *pt. s.* did, 75, 426, 858; Dede feteren, caused to be fettered, 866.

Deed, *pp.* dead, 69.

Deel, *s.* share, 635. A. S. *dǽl.*

Delen, *v.* divide, 18; *ger.* 43; Dele, *v.* 56; *ger.* 42; Deled, *pp.* 49; Deleth, *imp. pl.* 37. See Dalte. A. S. *dǽlan.*

Delyueraunce, *s.* gaol-delivery, 745.

Deme, *ger.* to condemn, 863. A. S. *déman,* from *dóm.*

Deyde, *pt. s.* died, 68.

Dight, *pp.* treated, served, 344, 730;

executed, 847; Yuel dight, in bad order, 87; Dighteth, *imp. pl.* get ready, 793. A. S. *dihtan,* borrowed from Lat. *dictare.*

Dismay 3ou, *imp. pl. refl.* be dismayed, 31; Dismaye the, *imp. s. refl.* be dismayed, 623, 763.

Do, *v.* cause, make, 158; *pr. s. subj.* may do, 492; Do on, *imp. s.* put on, 269; Do, *pp.* done, 144, 798. See Doon.

Dolfully, *adv.* dolefully, 475.

Domes, *pl.* judgments, sentences, 847, 870. A. S. *dóm.*

Doon, *v.* do, 207; *pp.* done, 211. A. S. *dón,* pp. *dón.* See Do.

Dore, *s.* door, 127.

Doughty, *adj.* brave, 2.

Doute, *s.* fear, 630.

Doutiden, *pt. pl.* feared, 78; Dowt, *imp. s.* fear, 517.

Dredden, *pt. pl.* dreaded, 309.

Dressen, *v.* to order, divide evenly, 18; re-arrange, 848; Dressed, *pp.* evenly divided, 15; Dresseth, *imp. pl.* divide evenly, 36. F. *dresser.*

Drewen hem awey, withdrew themselves, 308. See Drowe.

Dronke, *pt. pl.* drank, 681; *pp.* 334.

Drowe, *pt. pl.* drew backwards, 130. See Drewen.

Drye, *v.* to dry; With the wynde drye, to be dried by the wind, 880.

Dure, *v.* last, hold out, 831. F. *durer.*

Dwel, *imp. s.* dally, 579.

Dyner, *s.* dinner, 645.

E.

Eeke, *adv.* also, 480. A. S. *éac.*

Eeten, *pt. pl.* ate, 681.

Eighte, eighth, 331.

Elde, *s.* age, 649. A. S. *yldu,* age; from *eald,* old.

Elles, *adv.* else, 248. A. S. *elles.*

Endited, *pp.* indicted, 710.

Enquered, *pp.* enquired, 862.

Eny, any, 318.

Er, *adv.* ere, 568. See **Ar.**

Est, *s.* east, 891.

Euerich, each one, 443; each, 608; every one (of them), each, 119; Euerichone, every one, 866.

Eye, *s.* awe, 253 (see the note); Ey3e, 129 (see the note). A. S. *ege,* cognate with Icel. *agi* (whence E. *awe,* a Scand. form).

Eyr, *s.* heir, 40. O. F. *eir.*

F.

Fader, *s.* father, 7; Fadres, *gen.* 8, 886; Fader, *gen.* 748. A. S. *fæder.*

Fadmen, *s. pl.* fathoms, 306. The sing. is *fadme.* A. S. *fæðm,* Du. *vadem.*

Falle, *v.* happen, 485.

Fand, 1 *pt. s.* found, 206. See **Fond.** A. S. *fand,* pt. t. of *findan.*

Fare, *s.* behaviour, 199. A. S. *fær, faru,* sb.

Fare, *v.* fare, 271; *pr. s. subj.* may fare, 616. See **Ferde.** A. S. *faran.*

Fast aboute, very eager, 240, 785.

Fay, *s.* faith; By here fay, by their faith, 555. Anglo-F. *fei,* from Lat. acc. *fidem.*

Fayn, *adj.* glad, 103; *adv.* gladly, 15.

Feire, *s.* fair, i.e. business, 270. See the note.

Fel, *s.* skin, 76. A. S. *fel.*

Fel, *adj.* fell, cruel, 151, 256. A. S. *fel.*

Felaw, *s.* fellow, 227; (as a term of reproach), 276.

Felde, *pt. s.* felled, 593.

Fen, *s.* fen, mud, 588.

Ferd, *s.* fear, 854. This form occurs in Wyclif, Minot, Hampole's Prick of Conscience, and other poems (chiefly Northern).

Ferde, *pt. s.* fared, 780. See **Fare.**

Feteren, *ger.* to fetter, 384.

Feteres, *pl.* fetters, 384.

Fetten, *v.* fetch, 555; Fette, *ger.*

118; 2 *pr. pl.* 652; Fetteth, *imp. pl.* 643. A. S. *fetian.*

Fle, *v.* escape, 901.

Fley, *pt. s.* fled, 127. A. S. *fléah,* pt. t. of *fléon.*

Floon, *pl.* arrows, 648. A. S. *flá,* an arrow, pl. *flán;* also *flán,* an arrow, pl. *flána.* Icel. *fleinn.*

Flowe, *pp.* flown, fled, 133. See **Fley.** A. S. *flogen,* pp. of *fléah,* pt. t. of *fléon.*

Fond, *pt. s.* found, 610, 771, 773. See **Fand.**

Fondyng, *s.* trial, 147. A. S. *fandung,* a trial; from *fandian,* to try to find, try, tempt; der. from *fand,* pt. t. of *findan,* to find.

Foon, *pl.* foes, 541, 574. A. S. *fán,* pl. of *fá.*

For-fare, *v.* go to ruin, 74. A. S. *forfaran.*

Forgetith, *imp. pl.* forget, 38.

Forsworen, *pp.* perjured, 376, 380.

Forward, *s.* agreement, 411, 747. A. S. *fore-weard,* lit. a 'fore-ward,' i.e. precaution.

For3af, *pt. s.* forgave, 893.

For3at, *pt. s.* forgat, 800.

Foule, *adv.* evilly, 485.

Foy, faith; *par ma foy,* by my faith, 367. See **Fey.**

Frankeleyn, *s.* franklin, freeholder, 197. See Chaucer's Prologue.

Frere, *s.* friar, 529.

Fro, *prep.* from, 144. Icel. *frá.*

Fykil, *adj.* fickle, 151.

Fyn, *s.* end (of life), 551. F. *fin.*

Fyn, *adv.* finely, well, 681; excellently, 427.

G.

Gadelyng, *s.* companion, comrade (but used as a term of contempt, like vagabond), 102, 106. A. S. *gædeling,* a companion; Goth. *gadiliggs* (= *gadilings*), a relation; cf. G. *Gatte,* husband. Allied to E. *gather.*

Galys, Galicia, 277; Gales, 764. (In Spain).

Gamen, *s.* sport, a game, diversion, 290, 342; Game, amusement, pleasure, 776; sport, 4. A. S. *gamen.*

Gan, *pt. s.* did, 475. Lit. 'began,' but often used as a mere auxiliary verb. See **Gonne.**

Gerte, *pt. s.* struck (with a *yard* or stick), 304; struck, 536. From *gerden, girden,* verb; which from A. S. *gyrd, gierd,* a rod, stick, *yard.* See **Girde.**

Gestes, *pl.* guests, 336, 344, 640.

Geten, *pp.* gotten, 108, 365. A. S. *geten,* pp. of *gitan.*

Gilt, *s.* guilt, 893.

Giltyf, *adj.* guilty, 822; Gultyf, 824. A false form, the suffix *-if* being French.

Girde, *v.* strike, 430. See **Gerte.**

Gon, *v.* walk, 312. A. S. *gán.*

Gonne, *pt. pl.* (as aux. verb), did, 236. See **Gan.**

Good, *s.* property, 330. 704.

Goode, *voc.* O good, 199.

Goon, *v.* go, 236; *ger.* to go away, 126; Goth, *pr. s.* goes, 99; Goth, *imp. pl.* go ye, 36, 111, 713. A. S. *gán.*

Gowe, *for* go we, let us go, 661. So also in P. Plowman, prol. 226.

Grauen, *pp.* buried, 900. A. S. *grafen,* pp. of *grafan.*

Gray frere, a Gray friar, a Franciscan friar, 529.

Greeue, *s.* (*dat.*), grief, trouble, 313.

Greteth, *imp. pl.* greet ye, 713; Grette, *pt. pl.* saluted, greeted. 668, 706.

Grucche, *pr. s. subj.* murmur, 319. E. *grudge.*

Grucchyng, *s.* murmuring, grumbling, 322.

Gyle, *s.* guile, 369.

Gyled, *pt. s.* beguiled, 70.

H.

Hadde, I *pt. s. subj.* might have, 666; *pt. pl. subj.* might have, 16.

Halle dore, the door of the hall, 496; see note to l. 461.

Halp, I *pt. s.* helped, 60. A. S. *healp,* pt. t. of *helpan.*

Hals, *s.* neck, 391, 407. A. S. *heals.*

Haluendel, the half part (of), 272; see note. '*Haluendele* his godes he gaf to Godes werkes'; Rob. of Brunne, tr. of Langtoft, p. 24, l. 3.

Halues, *pl.* sides; By halues, on different sides, 130.

Handlen, *ger.* to handle, feel, 82.

Heed, *s.* head, 430, 484, 820; Heedes, *pl.* 602.

Heelden, *pt. pl.* accounted (themselves), 553.

Heere, 2 *pr. s. subj.* mayst hear, 229.

Heir, *s.* heir, 365. See **Eyr.**

Hele, *s.* good health, 41. A. S. *hǽlo,* health; from *hál,* whole.

Helpeth, *imp. pl.* help ye, 478.

Hem, *pron.* them, 15. A. S. *heom, him,* properly the dat. case. Still in use as *'em.*

Hende, *adj.* courteous, 663, 728, 755, 838. A. S. *gehende,* orig. handy, near at hand, from *hand,* hand.

Hente, *pt. s.* seized, took, 590, 591. A. S. *hentan.*

Hepe, *s.* heap; On an hepe, into a huddled crowd, 124.

Herden, *pt. pl.* heard, 21.

Here, *gen. pl.* of them, 543; their, 7, 757; Her, their, 43. A. S. *heora, hira,* of them; gen. pl. of *hé,* he.

Here, *v.* hear, 2.

Herkne, *imp. s.* hearken, 364; Herkneth, *imp. pl.* 858; Herkeneth, I.

Hete, *s.* heat of rage, 117.

Hider, *adv.* hither, 583. A. S. *hider.*

Highte, *pt. s.* was named, 727. A. S. *hátte,* I was called or named, pt. t. of *hátan* (1) to call, (2) to be named.

Hire, *adv.* here, 222. (A rare spelling).

Holde, *pp.* accounted, 248; Holdeth, *imp. pl.* hold ye, 169, 341, 769. A. S. *healden,* pp. of *healdan.*

Hond-fast, *adj.* fastened by the hands, 437.

Honge, *ger.* to hang, i.e. to be hanged, 863; Honged, *pt. pl.* hung, i.e. were hanged, 879.

Hore, *pl. adj.* hoary, gray, 817. A. S. *hár.*

Hosen, *pl.* hose, 269.

Housbond, *s.* husband, i.e. householder, one who stays at home and keeps house, 13 ; Housbondes, *pl.* labourers, men, 713.

Hure, *s.* hire, pay, 832. A. S. *hýr.*

Huyre, *ger.* to hire, 801 ; Hyre, 786. A.S. *hýran.*

Hye, *adv.* high, 879.

Hye, *v.* hasten away, 333 ; hasten, 19 ; Hyeden, *pt. pl. refl.* hied, hurried, 537.

I.

I-, prefix of past participles (and occasionally of past tenses) of verbs. Common in Southern, occasional in Midland, and unused in Northern poems. A. S. *ge-,* G. *ge-,* Goth. *ga-,* prefix. Also written *y-.*

Iame, James, 277, 665, 764.

I-bought, *pp.* bought, 278.

I-bounde, *pp.* bound, 350, 778. A. S. *gebunden,* pp. of *bindan.*

I-broken, *pp.* broken into, 85. A.S. *gebrocen,* pp. of *brecan.*

I-brought, *pp.* brought, 624.

I-come, *pp.* come, 459, 684.

I-crouned, *pp.* crowned, 660.

I-drawe, *pp.* drawn, dragged, pulled to the ground, 84. A.S. *gedragen,* pp. of *dragan.*

I-fetered, *pp.* fettered, 812.

I-go, *pp.* gone, ago, 257 ; I-gon, 356; I-goon, 347, 415. A. S. *gegán,* pp. of *gán.* (But E. *ago* = A. S. *á-gán*).

I-graue, *pp.* buried, 69. A. S. *gegrafen,* pp. of *grafan.*

I-had, *pp.* had, 357.

I-lad, *pp.* led, 884 ; carried, 528. The M. E. infin. is *leden.*

Ilke, same, 30.

I-lore, *pp.* lost, 301. A. S. *geloren,* pp. of *léosan,* M. E. *lesen.*

I-mad, *pp.* made, 689.

In-feere, *adv.* together, 517, 625, 667, 775, 866. For *in feere, in fere,* i.e. in companionship; formed from A. S. *ge-féra,* a travelling companion; der. from *fór,* pt. t. of *faran,* to travel, go.

I-nome, *pp.* taken, 119. A. S. *genumen,* pp. of *niman,* to take.

Iohan, John, 3, 57; saint John, 366.

Iolily, *adv.* in a jolly manner, merrily, 527.

I-pilt, *pp.* put, 894. Pp. of *pilten, pulten* (mod. E. *pelt*); from Lat. *pultare,* to beat, strike, knock.

I-proued, *pp.* proved, experienced, 241.

I-put, *pp.* put, thrust, 144.

I-schet, *pp.* shut, 292. A. S. *scyttan,* to shut.

I-set, *pp.* set, 857.

I-steke, *pp.* fastened up, 329. Pp. of M. E. *steken,* orig. to stick, pierce, pt. t. *stak.* Not found in A. S.

It ben, i. e. they are, 583.

I-taken, *pp.* taken, 350.

Iugge-man, *s.* judge, 843.

Iustise, *s.* judge, 890.

I-wounded, *pp.* wounded, 548.

I-wroken, *pp.* avenged, 541. A.S. *gewrocen,* pp. of *wrecan.*

I-wrought, *pp.* done, lit. worked, brought about, 32 ; Iwrou3t.

caused, 203. A.S. *geworht*, pp. of *wyrcan*.

I-wys, *adv.* certainly, 155, 411. A.S. *gewis*, adv. certainly; der. from *witan*, to know.

K.

Kiste, *pt. s.* kissed, 166, 168.
Knaue, *s.* boy, 70.

L.

Ladde, *pt. s.* led, 423. The infin. is *leden*. See **Ilad**.

Lakkest, 2 *pr. s.* blamest, 276. See the note. Cf. Du. *laken*, to blame; from *lak*, blemish, stain, defect.

Large, *adj.* liberal, 514. (The usual old sense; still preserved in *largesse*).

Largely, *adv.* liberally, 324; i.e. fully, completely, 520.

Lat, *imp. s.* 3 *p.* let, 112. See **Leet**.

Lawe, law; Of the beste lawe, in the best possible order, 544.

Laye, *adj.* fallow, 161. 'Lay, londe not telyd' [tilled]; Prompt. Parv.

Layen, *pt. pl.* lay, 83. A.S. *lǽgon*, pl. of *lǽg*, pt. t. of *licgan*.

Leche, *s.* physician, 614. A.S. *lǽce*.

Leede, *s.* people, serfs, 104, 895. A.S. *léod*, people. See below.

Leedes, *pl.* people, serfs; 'the portion of the population which was bought and sold with the land'; Wright. See l. 61; in l. 71, we have *leede*, i.e. people. This is the right *original* meaning. But it would seem that *leed* was afterwards extended to mean tenement or holding. Robert of Brunne seems to use *ledes* to mean tenements, rents, or fees. The phr. 'londes and ledes' occurs in Will. of Palerne, 4001, and is not uncommon. From A.S. *léod*, people.

Leet, *pt. s.* let, 74, 416; Leete, 1 *pr. s.* let, 405; Leet endite, caused to be indicted, 698; Leet fetre, caused to be fettered, 859; Leet sadle, caused to be saddled, 733; Leet vnfetere, caused to be unfettered, 837; Leet vp, *pt. s.* let up, i.e. opened, 311. A.S. *lǽtan*, to let, pt. t. *lét*, pp. *lǽten*.

Lendes, *pl.* loins, 458. A.S. *lendenu*, pl. the loins; Dan. *lend*, Swed. *länd*, loin.

Lene, *v.* lend, 176. A.S. *lǽnan*; from *lán*, a loan.

Lenger, *adv.* longer, 27, 337.

Lepe, *v.* run, 123. A.S. *hléapan*, to run.

Lese, *imp. s.* loose, 401. A.S. *lésan* or *lýsan*, to loose.

Leste, *adj.* least, 460.

Lesteneth, *imp. pl.* listen ye, 1, 169, 289, 341, 343, 551, 769.

Lesyng, *s.* lie, 659; Lesynges, *pl.* leasings, lies; Made lesynges on, told lies about, 385. A.S. *léasung*, a lie; from *léas*, false, loose.

Lete, *pt. pl.* let, left, 41; Leten, let, 46. See **Leet**.

Leue, *s.* leave, 314.

Leuer me were, it would be preferable for me, I would rather, 622. A.S. *léof*, dear.

Lewed, *adj.* ignorant, common, poor, 505. A.S. *lǽwede*.

Lewte, *s.* loyalty, fidelity, 657. Cf. F. *leauté*, loyalty, Cotgrave. From O. F. *leal*, Lat. *legalis*.

Leyde, *pt. s.* laid, 125; Leyd, *pp.* 162.

Lien, *v.* lie, be scattered about, 598. (See the note.) See **Lyen**.

Lighte, *pt. s.* alighted, 196, 611.

Litheth, *imp. pl.* hearken ye, listen ye, 1, 169, 289, 341, 769. Icel. *hlýða*, to listen, from *hljóð*, a sound. Allied to E. *loud*.

Lixt, 2 *pr. s.* liest, 297. So also in P. Plowman, B. v. 163.

Loft, *s.* loft, 127.

Loken, *ger.* to look, discover, 148 ; Lokede, *pt. s. subj.* should look, should observe, 642 ; Loke, *imp. s.* look, i.e. be ready, 453.

Lokkes, *pl.* locks of hair, 817.

Lond, *s.* land, 36, 104 ; Londes, *pl.* 18.

Lordynges, *pl.* sirs, 719.

Lore, *pp.* lost, 202. A. S. *loren,* pp. of *léosan.*

Lose, *v.* loose, 414. A. S. *losian,* See **Louse.**

Loth, *adj.* loath, 146.

Louse, *imp. s.* loose, 409. See **Lose.**

Lyen, *v.* lie, 41. See **Lien.**

Lytheth, 551. See **Litheth.**

Lyue, *dat.* ; On lyue, in life, a-live, 20, 58. Dat. of A. S. *líf,* life.

Lyuen, *v.* live, 12, 27 ; Lyuede, *pt. s.* lived, 9 ; Lyueden, *pt. pl.* 899.

Lyuerey, *s.* allowance, 514. 'Livrée, a delivery of a thing that is given, the thing so given, a livery.' Cotgrave.

M.

Mad, *pp.* made, 700.

Maister, *s.* master, 656, 658, 660 ; Maistres, *pl.* 314.

Makestow, 2 *pr. s.* makest thou, 199.

Maner men, manner of men, 312.

Mangerye, *s.* feast, 345, 434, 464. Also in P. Plowman, C. xiii. 46 ; and in Wyclif's Works, ed. Arnold, i. 4. Cotgrave gives F. *mangerie* with the sense of 'gluttony;' from *manger,* to eat.

Manly, *adv.* manfully, 832.

Martyn, St. Martin (see the note), 53, 225.

May, I *p. s. pr.* can, 27.

Mayn, *s.* main, might, 143.

Maynpris, *s.* bail, security, 744. See the note. Lit. 'a taking by the hand.' See note to P. Plowman, B. ii. 196.

Meede, *s.* reward, 886, 896.

Merthes, *pl.* diversions, amusements, 783.

Messager, *s.* messenger, 729.

Messes, *pl.* messes of meat, 467.

Meste, *adj.* greatest, 460.

Metten, *pt. pl.* met, 646.

Meyne, *s.* household, *posse,* company, 575. O.F. *mesnee, maisnee,* a household. Hence E. *menial.*

Mo, *adj.* more (in number), others, 260, 642, 736. A.S. *má.*

Moche, *adj.* great, 6, 230, 275. Used of size ; see below.

Mochel, *adj.* great, 400 ; Mochil, much, a great deal, 4. A.S. *mycel.*

Molde, *s.* mould, earth, 900. A.S. *molde.*

Moone, *s.* moon, 235. A.S. *móna.*

Moot, *s.* meeting, assembly, concourse, 373. See the note. A.S. *mót, gemót.*

Moot, I *pr. s.* may (I), 577 ; Moote, I *pr. pl.* ought (to be), must, 794. A.S. *mót,* I may, *pr. s.* ; *pt. t. móste* (= E. *must*). See **Mot.**

Moot-halle, hall of meeting, hall of justice, 812 ; Mote-halle, 717. See **Moot.**

More, *adj. comp.* greater, 232.

Most, 2 *pr. s.* must, 156, 242 ; Moste, *pt. s.* might, 724. See **Moot.**

Mot, I *pr. s.* may (I), 227, 379, 413 ; I must, 141 ; Mote, 2 *pr. s.* mayest, 233 ; Mot, 116 ; *pr. s.* may (it), 485 ; 2 *pr. pl.* may, 131. See **Moot.**

Mow, *pr. pl.* can, 675. As if for A.S. *mugon;* but the A.S. form is *magon.*

Myddeleste, *adj.* middlemost, i. e. second, 59.

Myle, *pl.* miles, 545. A.S. *míl,* pl. *míla.*

N.

Nam, *pt. s.* took, 733 ; *pt. pl.* took, 216. A.S. *nam,* pt. t. of *niman.*

Nas, *for* Ne was, was not, 29.

Nat, not, 37.

Nay, no; It is no nay, there is no denying it, 34; This is no nay, 433; Withoute nay, without denial, 26.

Ne, not, 30, 31; nor, 22, 79. A.S. *ne.*

Nedes, *adv.* needs, 846. Formed with adv. suffix *-es* from A.S. *néod, nýd,* need.

Neede, *adv.* of necessity, 141. Formed with adv. suffix *-e* from A.S. *néod,* need.

Neer, *adv.* nigher, 138, 352. See **Ner.**

Nekke, *s.* neck, 194. A.S. *knecca.*

Ner, *adv.* nigher, 109, 135. A.S. *néar,* compar. adv. from *néah,* nigh. See **Ny.**

Neyh, *adj.* nigh, 626. A.S. *néah.*

Neyhebours, *pl.* neighbours, 55. A.S. *néahgebúr.*

Nom, *var. of* Nim, *v.* take, 782 (*all the seven* MSS. *read* nom *or* nome); Nome, *pp.* taken, 584, 683, 796. A.S. *niman,* to take; *pp. genumen.*

Nones; With the nones = with then ones, with the once, on the condition, 206; For the nones, for the once, for the occasion, 456. (E. *nonce.*)

Norture, *s.* good breeding, 4.

Nother, *conj.* neither, 22.

Nothing, *adv.* not at all, 699.

Nought, *adv.* not at all, 31; not, 41.

Nowther, *conj.* neither, 79. See **Nother.**

Ny, *adj.* nigh, 559.

Nyggoun, *s.* niggard, 323. Spelt *nygun* in Rob. of Brunne, Handlyng Synne, 5578.

O.

O, *adj.* one, 371. See **Oo, Oon.**

Of, off, 196, 208, 484; *prep.* on, 217.

Oken, *adj.* oaken, 503.

Okes, *pl.* oaks, 84.

On lyue, alive, 157. See **Lyue.**

On, one; That on, the one, 39. See **Oon.**

Ones, *adv.* once, 234.

Oo, one, 150, 499. Short for *oon.*

Oon, one, 43, 244; At oon, at one, reconciled, 156, 166; That oon, the one of them, one of them, 647; the one (to be beaten), 116; On, one, 242. A.S. *án.*

Oones, *adv.* once; At oones, at once, soon, 141. A.S. *ánes.*

Or, *conj.* ere, 394. See **Ar.**

Ore, *s.* grace, favour; By Cristes ore, by the grace of Christ, 139, 159, 231, 323. A.S. *ár,* honour, favour; cf. G. *Ehre.*

Ote (a name), 727, 731, &c.

Other, *in phr.* day and other, one day and a second day, i. e. continually, 785. 'Notheles *day and other* he purueied priuely'; Rob. of Brunne, tr. of Langtoft, p. 185, l. 15.

Other, *conj.* either, 320.

Ouer-al, *adv.* everywhere, all round, 121. Cf. G. *überall.*

Overthrowe, *v.* fall down, stumble, 512; Ouerthrew, *pt. s.* fell down, 536.

Ow! *interj.* alas! 489.

P.

Paire, *s.* pair; Paire spores, pair of spurs, 188.

Pantrye, pantry, 495.

Parauenture, *adv.* perhaps, 642.

Parde, i. e. *par Dieu,* 743.

Parten. *pr. pl. subj.* (may) part, (may) depart, 317.

Party, *s.* party, person, 392.

Passe, 2 *pr. pl.* go away, depart, 596.

Pees, *s.* peace, 102.

Pestel, *s.* a pestle (apparently of large size, perhaps used for pounding meat, &c.), 122, 128. '*Pesteil*, a pestle, or pestell'; Cotgrave.

Peyned, *pt. s. refl.* took pains, 261.

Place, *s.* place for wrestling, place of public exhibition, the 'ring,' 195, 203, 210, 213, 216.

Pley3e, *ger.* play, make play, 130.

Plowes, *pl.* plough-lands, 57, 59, 358. 'A *plough* of land was as much as could be ploughed with one plough. It was in the middle ages a common way of estimating landed property'; Wright.

Prest, *adj.* ready, prepared, 237, 830. '*Prest*, prest, ready;' Cotgrave. O. F. *prest*, F. *prêt*.

Preuen, *v.* test, shew, 174. The same as Prouen.

Priue, *adj.* secret, 425.

Prouen, *v.* experience, 242.

Prow, *s.* profit, 361. O. F. *prou*, profit; supposed to be from Lat. *prod* in *prod-esse*, to benefit. Cf. Mod. E. *prowess.*

Prys, *s.* worth, valour, 772, 804.

Purchas, *s.* acquisition, 14, 61. See the note. '*Purchas*, is to buy lands or tenements with ones money, or otherwise gain them by ones industry, contradistinguished from that which comes to one by descent from his ancestors'; Blount, Law Dictionary. Doubtless the knight had partly won them as a reward for military service. See ll. 58-61.

Purs, *s.* purse, 321, 885. See the note to the latter line.

Pyn, *s.* bolt, bar, 292.

Q.

Quest, *s.* jury, 786, 862, 871, 878; in ll. 840, 842, it seems to mean the sentence or verdict. '*Queste*, a quest, inquirie'; Cotgrave.

Queste, *s.* bequest, 64.

Quitte, *pt. s.* repaid, 512, 896. '*Quiter*, to quit, forgoe, . . . discharge,' &c.; Cotgrave.

R.

Rape, *adj.* hasty, 101. Not a Latin, but a Scand. word. Icel. *hrapa*, to hasten; Swed. *rapp*, Dan. *rap*, quick.

Rapely, *adv.* quickly, 424; Raply, 219. See above.

Rede, 1 *pr. s.* advise, 605; 2 *pr. s. subj.* mayest advise, advisest, 797. A. S. *rǽdan* (E. *read*).

Reed, *s.* counsel, advice, 429, 432, 819; Reedes, *pl.* words of advice, 601. A. S. *rǽd.*

Rees, *s.* attack, 547; fit of passion, 101. A. S. *rǽs* (E. *race*). 'Griffyn, kyng of Wales, eft he *mad a res*'; Rob. of Brunne, tr. of Langtoft, p. 62, l. 16.

Rekke, *pr. s. subj.* may reck, may care, 881. See the note.

Reueth, *imp. pl.* reave ye, take away from, 111; Reued, *pp.* stolen away, 704. A. S. *reáfian.*

Rewe, *s.* (*dat.*) row, 867. A. S. *ráwe.*

Rewthe, *s.* pity, 508; Reuthe, 30. E. *ruth.* See Routhe.

Reysed, *pp.* raised, built, 162 Icel. *reisa.*

Richer, Richard, 175, 357, 619. See Rycher. Rob. of Brunne frequently writes *Richere* for Richard.

Rigge, *s.* back, 712. (E. *ridge*).

Rigge-boon, *s.* backbone, 614; Rigge-bon, 536.

Roode, *s.* (*dat.*), cross, 639, 707.

Roos, *pt. s.* arose, 849.

Route, *s.* company, 600; Rowte, 285.

Routhe, *s.* pity, 677. See Rewthe.

Rycher, Richard, 137. See the note. See Richer.

Ryue, *pl. adj.* rife, abundant, 783. Icel. *rífr.*

S.

Sadeled, *pp.* saddled, 187.

Saten, *pt. pl.* sat, 476.

Saugh, *pt. s.* saw, 134, 628. A.S. *seah.* See **Say.**

Saughte, *v.* be reconciled, come to terms, 150. From A.S. *saht,* reconciliation; der. from *sacan,* to dispute.

Say, *pt. s.* saw, 126, 494. See **Saugh.**

Schal, 1 *pr. s.* must, 115; *pr. s.* shall go, 326. A.S. *sceal.* See **Schulle.**

Schawes, *s. pl.* thickets, 788. A.S. *scaga;* cf. Icel. *skógr,* Swed. *skog,* Dan. *skov,* a shaw.

Scheete, *ger.* to shoot, 674. A.S. *scéotan.*

Schent, *pp.* put to shame, disgraced, 704. A.S. *scendan,* from *scand,* shame.

Scherreue, *s.* sheriff, 545, 602, 610, 611.

Schilde, *pr. s. imp.* may (He) shield, 767.

Schitte, *v.* shut, 286; *pt. s.* Schette, 127. A.S. *scyttan.*

Scholde, *pt. pl.* should, 12. See **Schulle.**

Schon, *pt. s.* shone, 235.

Schoon, *pl.* shoes, 208, 212, 269.

Schrewe, *s.* mischievous fellow, 230; wicked man, 6, 868.

Schulden, *pt. pl.* ought to, must, 19. A.S. *sceoldon,* pt. pl. of *sculan.*

Schulle, 1 *pr. pl.* are to, 156; Schul, must, are to, 158; Schulle, 2 *pr. pl.* shall, 2. A.S. *sculon,* pr. pl. of *sculan.*

Score, *s.* twenty, 628.

Seen, *ger.* to see, 146. A.S. *séonne,* ger. of *séon.*

Seet, *pt. s. subj.* should sit, 790.

A.S. *sǽte,* pt. s. subj. of *sittan,* pt. t. *sǽt.*

Seet, *s.* seat, 855.

Seih, *pt. s.* saw, 285. See **Seyh, Say.**

Selde, *adv.* seldom, 40. A.S. *seldan.*

Seller, *s.* cellar, 316.

Serk, *s.* shirt, 259. Icel. *serkr.*

Sete, *pt. pl.* sat, 681. A.S. *sǽton,* pt. pl. of *sittan.*

Seththen, *adv.* afterwards, 76. See **Siththen.**

Sette, *pt. pl.* set (themselves on knees, i. e. knelt), 705.

Seyh, *pt. s.* saw, 121, 299; Sey, 330. See **Saugh, Say.**

Sik, *adj.* sick, ill, 11, 21; Syk, 25.

Sire, *s.* master, 716.

Sisours, *pl.* jurymen, 871, 881. See note.

Sitte, *pr. s. subj.* sits, 761, 766, 794. Cf. *be* in l. 761.

Sith, *conj.* since, 257. See below.

Siththen, *adv.* afterwards, 524, 894; Sithen, 900. A.S. *siððám,* after that; cf. E. *sin-ce,* short for *sithen-ce.*

Siththen, *conj.* since that, 356.

Skape, *v.* escape, 576, 825.

Skathe, *s.* harm, 488.

Skeet, *adj.* swift; *hence as adv.* swiftly, quickly, 187. (Hence *Skeat* as a surname = swift.) A.S. *scéot,* Icel. *skjótr,* swift.

Slee, *v.* slay, 822.

Smertely, *adv.* quickly, 187, 243.

Solas, *s.* merriment, 328.

Sonde, *s.* sending; *hence,* providence, grace, 419. A.S. *sand,* a sending, mission; cf. mod. E. *godsend.*

Sone, *adv.* soon, 6, 67.

Sone, *s.* son, 38; Sones, *pl.* sons, 5. A.S. *sunu.*

Soneday, *s.* Sunday, 434.

Sope, *s.* sup, small quantity of drink, 318.

Soper, *s.* supper, 425.

Sore, *adv.* sorely, 10, 11.

Sory, *adj.* grievous, 547.

Sothe, *dat.* truth; For sothe, of a truth, 222.

Sowe, *pp.* sown, 161. A.S. *sáwen*, pp. of *sáwan*.

Spake, 2 *pt. s.* spakest, 94. A.S. *spréce*, 2 pt. s.; from *spræc*, 1 pt. s. of *sprecan*.

Spence, *s.* provision-room, larder, 424. 'Despence, a larder, store-house, gardemanger'; Cotgrave.

Spended, *pp.* spent, 362. 'Despendre, to dispend, spend'; Cotgrave.

Spense, *s.* expenditure, expense, 320. 'Despense. charge, cost, expence'; Cotgrave.

Spenser, *s.* spencer, officer who had charge of the provisions, 398, 399, 403; Spencer, 493. 'Despensier, a spender .. also a cater, or clarke of a Kitchin'; Cotgrave.

Spet, *pr. s.* (*short for* Spedeth), speeds, succeeds, goes on, 806.

Spire, *s.* a shoot, blade of grass; *hence*, a sapling, 503. A.S. *spír*, a spire, stalk; Icel. *spíra*, a spar, stilt; Dan. *spire*, a germ, sprout.

Spores, *pl.* spurs, 177, 188. A.S. *spura*.

Sprengeth, *pr. s.* sprinkles, 503. Cf. A.S. *besprengan*, to besprinkle.

Staf, staff, 499; Staves, staves, 496.

Stalkede, *pt. s.* marched, 617.

Stalworthe, *adj. pl.* stalwart, lusty, 202.

Standeth, *imp. pl.* Stand ye, 55; Stant (*for* Standeth), *pr. s.* stands, 812.

Stede, *s.* stead, place, 425, 857.

Stere, *imp. s. refl.* stir thyself, 519.

Sterte, *pt. s.* started, 219, 288; Sterten, *pt. pl.* 645.

Stoon-stille, *adj.* still as a stone, 67. See the note.

Stoor, *s.* store, 354.

Stounde, *s.* time, while, 349; In this stounde, at the present hour, 27. A.S. *stund*; cf. G. *Stunde*.

Strengest, *adj.* strongest, 78. A.S. *strengest*, superl. of *strang*, strong.

Stronge, *adv.* strongly, 397.

Stroye, *ger.* to destroy, waste, 354. Short for *destroye*.

Styrop, *s.* stirrup, 189. A.S. *stigráp*.

Swaynes, *pl.* servants, 527. Icel. *sveinn*, a boy, lad, servant; A.S. *swán*.

Sweere, *s.* neck, 274. A.S. *sweora*.

Swithe, *adv.* very, 152; As swithe, as soon, 541. A.S. *swiðe*, adv. very; from *swið*, strong.

Swore, *pp.* sworn, 302. See the note. A.S. *sworen*, pp. of *swerian*.

T.

Take, 1 *pr. s.* deliver, 747.

Talkyng, *s.* talk, tale, 2, 170.

Teene, *s.* vexation, anger, rage, 303. A.S. *téona*, injury.

Telle, *v.* count, 520.

Thanne, *adv.* then, 652.

That, *rel.* that which, 324.

That on, the one; That other, the other, 39.

Thee, *v.* thrive, prosper, 131, 250; The, *v.* 234, 363, 379, 413, 458, 577, 720, 833. A.S. *þéon*, cognate with G. *gedeihen*.

Thenke, 2 *pr. s. subj.* thinkest, intendest, 368. A.S. *þencan*, to think.

Thennes, *adv.* thence, 535.

Ther, *adv.* where, 11, 25, 33, 50, 195, 471, 799; Ther .. inne, wherein, 558. A.S. *þær*.

Therfor, for it, i.e. as a prize for it, 184.

They, *conj.* though, 652. A.S. *þéah*.

Thider, *adv.* thither, 123, 310, 527. A.S. *þider*.

Thinketh me, *pr. s. impers.* it seems to me, 95. A.S. *þyncan*, impers. to seem.

Tho, then, 17, 41, 110; when, 21, 120, 372. A. S. *ðá*, when; also, then.

Tho, *pron.* those, 279. A. S. *ðá*, pl. of *se, séo, þæt*, used as def. art.

Thought, *pt. s.* it seemed (to him), 626. See **Thinketh**.

Thridde, *adj.* third, 687. A. S. *þridda*.

Thrynne (*for* Therynne), therein, in it, 318.

Thryue, *v.* thrive, 227.

Thurgh, *prep.* through, by, 28.

Thynketh, *pr. s.* it seems (to me), 632. See **Thinketh**.

To, *adv.* too, 278.

To-barst, *pt. s.* burst in twain, was broken in half, 537. (It merely means that the skin above the backbone was broken; formerly, a 'broken head' meant only that the skin was cut through, not that the skull was fractured.) A. S. *tóbærst*, pt. t. of *tó-berstan*.

To-brak, *pt. s.* brake in twain, 304, 852. A. S. *tóbræc*, pt. t. of *tó-brecan*, to break in twain. See below.

Tobrak, *pt. pl.* brake in twain, 245. (Should be the pl. *tobreke*. Grammar would be better satisfied if we could take it to mean 'that he brake in twain three of his ribs.')

To-broken, *pp.* broken into, 97. A. S. *tóbrocen*, pp. of *tó-brecan*. See **To-brak**.

Tonge, *s.* tongue, 169, 341. A. S. *tunge*.

Tonne, *as pl.* tuns, 316. A. S. *tunne*, a barrel.

Toret, *s.* turret, 329.

To-rightes, *adv.* aright, rightly, 18. We still say 'to set to-rights.' The suffix *-es* is adverbial.

Tornes, *pl.* turns, tricks, wiles, 237, 241, 244.

Tweyne, two, 734; Tweye, two,

202. A. S. *twegen*, masc.; *twá*, fem. and neuter.

Twynke, 1 *pr. s.* wink, 453. 'Twynkyn wythe the eye, or wynkyn, twynkelyn, *conniveo, nicito, nicto*'; Prompt. Parv.

V.

Verrey, *adj.* very, real, 14. See note.

Vilonye, *s.* disgrace, 721.

Vnfetered, *pt. s.* released from his fetters, 613.

Ungert, *pp.* ungirt, 215.

Vnhiled, *pp.* unroofed, uncovered, 87. Icel. *hylja*, to cover. Cf. A. S. *helan*, to cover. 'Hyllyn, hyllen, coueren, *Operio, tego*'; Prompt. Parv.

Vnloke, *pp.* unlocked, 438. See the note. A. S. *locen*, pp. of *lúcan*, to lock.

Vnsawe, *pp.* unsown, 83. A. S. *sáwen*, pp. of *sáwan*, to sow.

Vp, *prep.* upon, 411.

W.

Wan, *pt. s.* won, begot, 5. A. S. *wann*, pt. t. of *winnan*.

War, *adj.* aware, 122, 497. A. S. *wær*.

Wardeynes, *pl.* wardens, umpires, 279.

Ware, *s.* merchandise, 272, 276.

Wasschen, *pp.* washen, 439. A. S. *wascen*, pp. of *wascan*.

Wayloway, *interj.* wellaway! 197. For A. S. *wá lá wá*, lit. 'woe! lo! woe!'

Waynes, *pl.* wains, 528.

Wede, *s.* raiment, 103. A. S. *wǽd*.

Wende, *v.* go, 756; *ger.* to go, 173, 340; *imp. s.* 213; Went, *pp.* turned, 703.

Wene, 1 *pr. s.* suppose, think, 202.

Were. *pt. s. subj.* would be, 146.

Werche, *v.* work, 518.

Werne, *v.* refuse, 662; *pr. pl.* refuse, deny, 457. A. S. *wyrnan*, to refuse. Allied to E. *warn*.

Weyuen, *ger.* to dangle, to swing about, 880. Icel. *veifa*, to vibrate, Norweg. *veiva*, to swing about.

What, *adv.* partly, 543. Cf. mod. E. '*what* with one thing and *what* with another.'

What, why, 104.

Wher, *conj.* whether (shall I go), 430. Contracted form of *whether*.

Whether, which ever, 249.

Which, what (sort of), 168.

Whider, *adv.* whither, 133, 182. A. S. *hwider*.

Wight, *s.* man, 107. A. S. *wiht*.

Wighte, *adj. pl.* active, 893. Cf. Icel. *vigr*, skilled in arms; Swed. *vig*, active (whence *vigt*, adv. nimbly).

Wil, *s.* will; Of good wil, readily, 78 (see note); In good wil, anxious, 173.

Wil, *pr. s.* desires, 262; Wilt, 2 *pr. s.* wishest, 207; Wiln, 1 *pr. pl.* will, 314, 821.

Wisschen, *pt. pl.* washed themselves, 542. (More commonly *weschen* or *woschen*).

Wiste, *pt. s.* knew, 167, 369, 864; Wist, *pp.* 393. A. S. *wiste*, pt. t. of *witan*. (The A. S. pp. was *witen*). See below.

Witen, *ger.* to know, ascertain, 572; 1 *pr. pl. subj.* may know, 644. A. S. *witan*; pr. pl. subj. *witon*. See above.

Withoute, *adv.* outside, 286, 854; on the outside, 564.

Wo, *adj.* sorry, 335. Cf. Ch. Prol. 353. This use of *wo* arose from putting ' he was wo ' for ' him was wo '; *wo* being orig. a sb.

Wolde, *pt. s.* willed (it to be so), 899; desired, 15.

Wolt, 2 *pr. s.* wilt, wishest to, 182.

Wolues-heed, *s.* wolf's-head, proscribed as an outlaw, 700, 710, 722. See note to l. 700.

Wonderly, *adv.* wonderfully, 266.

Wood, *adj.* mad, 386, 472. A. S. *wód*, mad.

Woode-bow3, *s.* boughs of the wood, 633; Woode-bough, 774.

Woode-lynde, *s.* a linden-tree in a forest, 676, 702. A. S. *lind*, a linden or lime-tree.

Woode-rys, *s.* thicket, branches of the forest, 771, 803. A. S. *hrís* (Icel. *hrís*, Dan. *riis*, Swed. *ris*, G. *reis*), brushwood. Lit. ' waving boughs '; cf. Goth. *hrisjan*, to shake.

Woode-schawe, *s.* thicket of the wood, 638; Woode-schawes, *pl.* 670, 696. See Schawes.

Woon, *s.* abundance; Good-woon, abundantly, 125. ' Woone, or grete plente, *Copia, habundantia* '; Prompt. Parv.

Worschip, *s.* honour, 185.

Worthe, *v.* be, 491; *imp. s. 3 p.* may (it) be, 482. A. S. *weorðan*, to be, become.

Wot, 1 *pr. s.* know, 34. A. S. *wát*, pr. t. of *witan*.

Woxe, *pp.* waxen, grown, 232. A. S. *waxen, weaxen*, pp. of *weaxan*.

Wrak, *pt. s.* wreaked, 303; avenged (himself), 896. A. S. *wræc*, pt. t. of *wrecan*.

Wrastled, 1 *pt. s.* wrestled, 257. A. S. *wrǽstlian*.

Wrastlyng, *s.* wrestling-match, 171, 183; Wrastelyng, 190, 194.

Wraththe, *v.* make angry, 80; Wraththed him, *pt. s.* grew angry, 91.

Wreke, *pp.* avenged, 346. A. S. *wrecen*, pp. of *wrecan*.

Wrothe, *adv.* evilly, ill (lit. perversely), 73. In Rob. of Glouc., ed. Hearne, p. 31, Lear complains that Cordelia returns his love *wroþe*, i. e. evilly.

Wroughte, *pt. pl.* worked, 525; Wrought, *pp.* done, 51. A. S. *worhte*, pt. t. of *wyrcan*; pp. *geworht*.

Wurs, *adv.* worse, 740.

Wyde-wher, *adv.* far and wide, in various lands, 13.

Wyf, *pl.* wives, 713. See the note.

Wyke, *s.* week, 687. A.S. *wice, wicu*; also spelt *wuce, wucu*.

Wyt, *s.* wisdom, wittiness, 111. (Not wits, senses.)

Y.

Y-, prefix; see **I-**, prefix.

Yat, *s.* gate, 293. See **ʒate**.

Y-bounde, *pp.* bound, 397, 606. A.S. *gebunden*, pp. of *bindan*.

•**Y-doon**, *pp.* done, 54; Y-don, 529, ended, 846. A.S. *gedón*, pp. of *dón*.

Y-dronke, *pp.* drunk, 428. A.S. *gedruncen*, pp. of *drincan*.

Yě, *s.* eye, 334. A.S. *éage*.

Yeer, *pl.* years, 404; Yer, 358. A.S. *géar*, a year; pl. *géar*. See **ʒeer**.

Yemede, *pt. pl.* took care of, guarded, 267. A.S. *gýman, géman*, to take care of; Goth. *gaumjan*, to heed.

Y-fetered, *pp.* fettered, 612.

Y-founde, *pp.* found out, invented, 393. A.S. *gefunden*, pp. of *findan*.

Ying, *adj.* young, 105, 148. See **ʒing**.

Y-nome, *pp.* taken, 741. A.S. *genumen*, pp. of *niman*.

Y-prisoned, *pp.* cast into prison, 737.

Y-steke, *pp.* fastened, 563. See **I-steke**.

Y-told, *pp.* told, 546.

Yuel, *adv.* ill, badly, 73, 448.

Y-ʒeue, *pp.* given, 870. See **ʒeue**.

ʒ.

ʒaf, *pt. s.* gave, 246, 500. A.S. *geaf*, pt. t. of *gifan*.

ʒare, *adj.* ready, 90. A.S. *gearo, gearu*, ready, prompt.

ʒare, *adv.* quickly, 793. See above. Shak. has *yare*.

ʒate, *s.* gate, 579. A.S. *geat*.

ʒe, *adv.* yea, 447.

ʒede, *pt. s.* went, 243, 311, 352; ʒeeden, *pt. pl.* 510. A.S. *geéode*, went.

ʒeer, *pl.* years, 361. See **Yeer**.

ʒelde, 3 *p. pr. s. imper.* (may God) requite, repay, 368; Yeldeth, *imp. pl.* yield ye, give up, 648.

ʒeme, *s.* heed, care, 825. See **Yemede**.

ʒerde, *s.* yard, court of a mansion, 81, 296. A.S. *geard*, an enclosure.

ʒeue, *v.* give, 48, 205; ʒeuen, *pp.* given, 456, 847; ʒeue, *pp.* 394. A.S. *gifan, giefan*; pp. *gifen, giefen*.

ʒif, *imp. s.* 5 *p.* may (God) give, 551. See **ʒeue**.

ʒif, *conj.* if, 158. A.S. *gif*, if; which probably stands for *ge-if*, i.e. *if* with the prefix *ge-*. For compare Icel. *ef*, O. Icel. *if*, if.

ʒing, *adj.* young, 887. See **ʒonge**. The spelling *ging* is found occasionally in A.S.; *ʒing* is in Rob. of Brunne, tr. of Langtoft, p. 95, l. 10.

ʒonder, *adv.* yonder, 641.

ʒonge, *adj.* young, 38, 70.

ʒongest, *adj.* youngest, 44.

ʒore, *adv.* for a long while, long since, 257, 324; a long time, 9. (E. *yore*).

ʒow, *pron.* acc. you, 63; ʒou, 200. A.S. *éow*.

THE END.

Clarendon Press Series.

The English Language and Literature.

HELPS TO THE STUDY OF THE LANGUAGE.

1. DICTIONARIES.

A NEW ENGLISH DICTIONARY ON HISTORICAL PRIN-CIPLES, founded mainly on the materials collected by the Philological Society. Imperial 4to. Parts I-IV, price 12s. 6d. each.

Vol. I (A and B), half-morocco, 2l. 12s. 6d.

Vol. II (C and D). *In the Press.*

Part IV, Section 2, **C—CASS**, beginning Vol. II, price 5s.

Part V, **CAST—CLIVY**, price 12s. 6d.

Part VI, **CLO—CONSIGNER**, price 12s. 6d.

Part VII, **CONSIGNIFICANT—CROUCHING.** Price 12s. 6d.

Edited by JAMES A. H. MURRAY, LL.D., sometime President of the Philological Society; with the assistance of many Scholars and Men of Science.

Vol. III (E, F, G), Part I, **E—EVERY**, Edited by HENRY BRADLEY, M.A., price 12s. 6d.

Bosworth and **Toller.** *An Anglo-Saxon Dictionary,* based on the MS. Collections of the late JOSEPH BOSWORTH, D.D. Edited and enlarged by Prof. T. N. TOLLER, M.A. Parts I-III, A-SAR. . . . [4to, 15s. each.

Part IV, Section I, SÁR—SWÍÐRIAN. . . . . [4to, 8s. 6d.

Mayhew and **Skeat.** *A Concise Dictionary of Middle English,* from A. D. 1150 to 1580. By A. L. MAYHEW, M.A., and W. W. SKEAT, Litt.D.
[Crown 8vo, half-roan, 7s. 6d.

Skeat. *A Concise Etymological Dictionary of the English Language.* By W. W. SKEAT, Litt.D. *Fourth Edition.* . . [Crown 8vo, 5s. 6d.

B

2. GRAMMARS, READING BOOKS, &c.

Earle. *The Philology of the English Tongue.* By J. EARLE, M.A., Professor of Anglo-Saxon. *Fifth Edition.* . . [Extra fcap. 8vo, 8s. 6d.

———— *A Book for the Beginner in Anglo-Saxon.* By J. EARLE, M.A., Professor of Anglo-Saxon. *Third Edition.* . . [Extra fcap. 8vo, 2s. 6d.

Mayhew. *Synopsis of Old-English Phonology.* By A. L. MAYHEW, M.A. . . : . . . [Extra fcap. 8vo, bevelled boards, 8s. 6d.

Morris and **Skeat.** *Specimens of Early English:*—

Part I. From Old English Homilies to King Horn (A.D. 1150 to A.D. 1300). By R. MORRIS, LL.D. *Second Edition.* . . [Extra fcap. 8vo, 9s.

Part II. From Robert of Gloucester to Gower (A.D. 1298 to A.D. 1393). By R. MORRIS, LL.D., and W. W. SKEAT, Litt.D. *Third Edition.* 7s. 6d.

Skeat. *Specimens of English Literature*, from the 'Ploughmans Crede' to the 'Shepheardes Calender.' . . [Extra fcap. 8vo, 7s. 6d.

———— *The Principles of English Etymology:*

First Series. The Native Element. *Second Edition.* [Crown 8vo, 10s. 6d.

Second Series. The Foreign Element. . . . [Crown 8vo, 10s. 6d.

———— *A Primer of English Etymology.* [Extra fcap. 8vo, *stiff covers*, 1s. 6d.

Sweet. *A New English Grammar, Logical and Historical.* Part I. Introduction, Phonology, and Accidence. . . . [Crown 8vo, 10s. 6d.

———— *A Short Historical English Grammar.* [Extra fcap. 8vo, 4s. 6d.

———— *A Primer of Historical English Grammar.* [Extra fcap. 8vo, 2s.

———— *History of English Sounds from the Earliest Period.* With full Word-Lists. . . . . [8vo, 14s.

———— *An Anglo-Saxon Primer, with Grammar, Notes, and Glossary.* By HENRY SWEET, M.A. *Third Edition.* . . [Extra fcap. 8vo, 2s. 6d.

———— *An Anglo-Saxon Reader.* In Prose and Verse. With Grammatical Introduction, Notes, and Glossary. By the same Author. *Sixth Edition, Revised and Enlarged.* . . . . [Extra fcap. 8vo, 8s. 6d.

———— *A Second Anglo-Saxon Reader.* By the same Author. [4s. 6d.

———— *Old English Reading Primers.* By the same Author:—

I. *Selected Homilies of Ælfric.* [Extra fcap. 8vo, *stiff covers*, 1s. 6d.

II. *Extracts from Alfred's Orosius.* [Extra fcap. 8vo, *stiff covers*, 2s.

———— *First Middle English Primer, with Grammar and Glossary.* By the same Author. *Second Edition* . . . . [Extra fcap. 8vo, 2s.

———— *Second Middle English Primer.* Extracts from Chaucer, with Grammar and Glossary. By the same Author. . [Extra fcap. 8vo, 2s. 6d.

———— *A Primer of Spoken English.* . . [Extra fcap. 8vo, 3s. 6d.

———— *A Primer of Phonetics.* . . . [Extra fcap. 8vo, 3s. 6d.

———— *A Manual of Current Shorthand, Orthographic and Phonetic.* [4s. 6d.

Tancock. *An Elementary English Grammar and Exercise Book.* By O. W. TANCOCK, M.A. *Second Edition.* . . [Extra fcap. 8vo, 1s. 6d.

———— *An English Grammar and Reading Book,* for Lower Forms in Classical Schools. By O. W. TANCOCK, M.A. *Fourth Edition.* [3s. 6d.

Twelve Facsimiles of Old-English Manuscripts. . [4to, 7s. 6d.

A SERIES OF ENGLISH CLASSICS.

(CHRONOLOGICALLY ARRANGED.)

Chaucer. I. *The Prologue to the Canterbury Tales. (School Edition.)* Edited by W. W. SKEAT, Litt.D. . . [Extra fcap. 8vo, *stiff covers*, 1s.

—— II. *The Prologue; The Knightes Tale; The Nonne Prestes Tale.* Edited by R. MORRIS, LL.D. *A New Edition, with Collations and Additional Notes,* by W. W. SKEAT, Litt.D. . . [Extra fcap. 8vo, 2s. 6d.

—— III. *The Prioresses Tale; Sir Thopas; The Monkes Tale; The Clerkes Tale; The Squieres Tale, &c.* Edited by W. W. SKEAT, Litt.D. *Fourth Edition.* . . . . . [Extra fcap. 8vo, 4s. 6d.

—— IV. *The Tale of the Man of Lawe; The Pardoneres Tale; The Second Nonnes Tale; The Chanouns Yemannes Tale.* By the same Editor. *New Edition, Revised.* . . . [Extra fcap. 8vo, 4s. 6d.

—— V. *Minor Poems.* By the same Editor. [Crown 8vo, 10s. 6d.

—— VI. *The Legend of Good Women.* By the same Editor. [Crown 8vo, 6s.

Langland. *The Vision of William concerning Piers the Plowman,* by WILLIAM LANGLAND. Edited by W. W. SKEAT, Litt.D. *Fourth Edition.* [Extra fcap. 8vo, 4s. 6d.

Gamelyn, The Tale of. Edited by W. W. SKEAT, Litt.D. [Extra fcap. 8vo, *stiff covers*, 1s. 6d.

Wycliffe. *The New Testament in English,* according to the Version by JOHN WYCLIFFE, about A.D. 1380, and Revised by JOHN PURVEY, about A.D. 1388. With Introduction and Glossary by W. W. SKEAT, Litt.D. [Extra fcap. 8vo, 6s.

—— *The Books of Job, Psalms, Proverbs, Ecclesiastes, and the Song of Solomon:* according to the Wycliffite Version made by NICHOLAS DE HEREFORD, about A.D. 1381, and Revised by JOHN PURVEY, about A.D. 1388. With Introduction and Glossary by W.W.SKEAT, Litt.D. [Extra fcap. 8vo, 3s. 6d.

Minot. *The Poems of Laurence Minot.* Edited, with Introduction and Notes, by JOSEPH HALL, M.A. . . . . [Extra fcap. 8vo, 4s. 6d.

Spenser. *The Faery Queene.* Books I and II. Edited by G. W. KITCHIN, D.D., with Glossary by A. L. MAYHEW, M.A.

     Book I. *Tenth Edition.* . . . . . [Extra fcap. 8vo, 2s. 6d.
     Book II. *Sixth Edition.* . . . . . [Extra fcap. 8vo, 2s. 6d.

Hooker. *Ecclesiastical Polity,* Book I. Edited by R. W. CHURCH, M.A., late Dean of St. Paul's. *Second Edition.* . . [Extra fcap. 8vo, 2s.

Marlowe and **Greene.** MARLOWE'S *Tragical History of Dr. Faustus,* and GREENE'S *Honourable History of Friar Bacon and Friar Bungay.* Edited by A. W. WARD, Litt.D. *Third Edition.* . . [Crown 8vo, 6s. 6d.

Marlowe. *Edward II.* Edited by O. W. TANCOCK, M.A. *Second Edition.* . . . . . [Extra fcap. 8vo. *Paper covers*, 2s.; cloth, 3s.

Shakespeare. Select Plays. Edited by W. G. CLARK, M.A., and W. ALDIS WRIGHT, D.C.L. . . . . [Extra fcap. 8vo, *stiff covers.*

> The Merchant of Venice. 1s.   Macbeth. 1s. 6d.
> Richard the Second. 1s. 6d.   Hamlet. 2s.

Edited by W. ALDIS WRIGHT, D.C.L.

> The Tempest. 1s. 6d.   Coriolanus. 2s. 6d.
> As You Like It. 1s. 6d.   Richard the Third. 2s. 6d.
> A Midsummer Night's Dream. 1s. 6d.   Henry the Fifth. 2s.
> Twelfth Night. 1s. 6d.   King John. 1s. 6d.
> Julius Cæsar. 2s.   King Lear. 1s. 6d.
>   Henry the Eighth. 2s.

Shakespeare as a Dramatic Artist; *a popular Illustration of the Principles of Scientific Criticism.* By R. G. MOULTON, M.A. [Cr. 8vo, 7s. 6d.

Bacon. *Advancement of Learning.* Edited by W. ALDIS WRIGHT, D.C.L. *Third Edition.* . . . . . [Extra fcap. 8vo, 4s. 6d.

—— *The Essays.* Edited, with Introduction and Illustrative Notes, by S. H. REYNOLDS, M.A. . . . . [Demy 8vo, *half-bound,* 12s. 6d.

Milton. I. *Areopagitica.* With Introduction and Notes. By JOHN W. HALES, M.A. *Third Edition.* . . . . [Extra fcap. 8vo, 3s.

—— II. *Poems.* Edited by R. C. BROWNE, M.A. In two Volumes. *Fifth Edition.*
[Extra fcap. 8vo, 6s. 6d. Sold separately, Vol. I. 4s., Vol. II. 3s.
In paper covers:—
> Lycidas, 3d.   L'Allegro, 3d.   Comus, 6d.

By OLIVER ELTON, B.A.
> Lycidas, 6d.   L'Allegro, 4d.   Il Penseroso, 4d.   Comus, 1s.

—— III. *Paradise Lost.* Book I. Edited with Notes, by H. C. BEECHING, M.A. . . [Extra fcap. 8vo, 1s. 6d. *In Parchment,* 3s. 6d.

—— IV. *Paradise Lost.* Book II. Edited by E. K. CHAMBERS, B.A. . . . [Extra fcap. 8vo, 1s. 6d. Books I and II together, 2s. 6d.

—— V. *Samson Agonistes.* Edited, with Introduction and Notes, by JOHN CHURTON COLLINS, M.A. . . [Extra fcap. 8vo, *stiff covers,* 1s.

Milton's Prosody. By ROBERT BRIDGES. [Small 4to, 8s. 6d. net.

Bunyan. I. *The Pilgrim's Progress, Grace Abounding, Relation of the Imprisonment of Mr. John Bunyan.* Edited by E. VENABLES, M.A.
[Extra fcap. 8vo, 3s. 6d. *In Parchment,* 4s. 6d.

—— II. *The Holy War, and the Heavenly Footman.* Edited by MABEL PEACOCK. . . . . [Extra fcap. 8vo, 3s. 6d.

Clarendon. *Selections.* Edited by G. BOYLE, M.A., Dean of Salisbury. . . . . [Crown 8vo, 7s. 6d.

Dryden. *Select Poems.* (*Stanzas on the Death of Oliver Cromwell; Astræa Redux; Annus Mirabilis; Absalom and Achitophel; Religio Laici; The Hind and the Panther.*) Edited by W. D. CHRISTIE, M.A. *Fifth Edition.* Revised by C. H. FIRTH, M.A. . . . [Extra fcap. 8vo, 3s. 6d.

—— *Essay of Dramatic Poesy.* Edited, with Notes, by T. ARNOLD, M.A. . . . . [Extra fcap. 8vo, 3s. 6d.

Locke. *Conduct of the Understanding.* Edited, with Introduction, Notes, &c., by T. FOWLER, D.D. *Third Edition.* . [Extra fcap. 8vo, 2s. 6d.

Addison. *Selections from Papers in the 'Spectator.'* By T. ARNOLD, M.A. *Sixteenth Thousand.* . [Extra fcap. 8vo, 4s. 6d. *In Parchment,* 6s.

Steele. *Selected Essays from the Tatler, Spectator, and Guardian.* By AUSTIN DOBSON. . . . [Extra fcap. 8vo, 5s. *In Parchment,* 7s. 6d.

Swift. *Selections from his Works.* Edited, with Life, Introductions, and Notes, by HENRY CRAIK. Two Vols. [Crown 8vo, cloth extra, price 15s. *Each volume may be had separately, price 7s. 6d.*

Pope. I. *Essay on Man.* Edited by MARK PATTISON, B.D. *Sixth Edition.* . . . . [Extra fcap. 8vo, 1s. 6d.

—— II. *Satires and Epistles.* By the same Editor. *Second Edition.* [Extra fcap. 8vo, 2s.

Thomson. *The Seasons,* and *The Castle of Indolence.* Edited by J. LOGIE ROBERTSON, M.A. . . . . [Extra fcap. 8vo, 4s. 6d.

—— *The Castle of Indolence.* By the same Editor. [Extra fcap. 8vo, 1s. 6d.

Berkeley. *Selections.* With Introduction and Notes. By A. C. FRASER, LL.D. *Fourth Edition.* . . . . . [Crown 8vo, 8s. 6d.

Johnson. I. *Rasselas.* Edited, with Introduction and Notes, by G. BIRKBECK HILL, D.C.L. [Extra fcap. 8vo, *limp,* 2s. ; *Bevelled boards,* 3s. 6d. ; *in Parchment,* 4s. 6d.

—— II. *Rasselas; Lives of Dryden and Pope.* Edited by ALFRED MILNES, M.A. . . . . . [Extra fcap. 8vo, 4s. 6d.

Lives of Dryden and Pope. . . [Stiff covers, 2s. 6d.

—— III. *Life of Milton.* Edited, with Notes, &c., by C. H. FIRTH, M.A. . . . [Extra fcap. 8vo, *stiff covers,* 1s. 6d. ; *cloth,* 2s. 6d.

—— IV. *Vanity of Human Wishes.* With Notes, by E. J. PAYNE, M.A. . . . . [Paper covers, 4d.

Gray. *Selected Poems.* Edited by EDMUND GOSSE, M.A. [In Parchment, 3s.

—— *The same,* together with Supplementary Notes for Schools. By FOSTER WATSON, M.A. . . . [Extra fcap. 8vo, *stiff covers,* 1s. 6d.

—— *Elegy, and Ode on Eton College.* . . . [Paper covers, 2d.

Goldsmith. *Selected Poems.* Edited, with Introduction and Notes, by AUSTIN DOBSON . . [Extra fcap. 8vo, 3s. 6d. *In Parchment,* 4s. 6d.

—— *The Traveller.* Edited by G. B. HILL, D.C.L. [Stiff covers, 1s.

—— *The Deserted Village.* . . . . . [Paper covers, 2d.

Cowper. I. *The Didactic Poems of* 1782, with Selections from the Minor Pieces, A.D. 1779–1783. Edited by H. T. GRIFFITH, B.A. [Extra fcap. 8vo, 3s.

—— II. *The Task, with Tirocinium,* and Selections from the Minor Poems, A.D. 1784–1799. By the same Editor. [Extra fcap. 8vo, 3s.

Burke. I. *Thoughts on the Present Discontents ; the two Speeches on America.* Edited by E. J. PAYNE, M.A. . . [Extra fcap. 8vo, 4s. 6d.

—— II. *Reflections on the French Revolution.* By the same Editor. *Second Edition.* . . . . . [Extra fcap. 8vo, 5s.

—— III. *Four Letters on the Proposals for Peace with the Regicide Directory of France.* By the same Editor. [Extra fcap. 8vo, 5s.

Burns. *Selected Poems.* Edited by J. LOGIE ROBERTSON, M.A.
[Crown 8vo, 6s.

Keats. *Hyperion*, Book I. With Notes, by W. T. ARNOLD, B.A. 4d.

Byron. *Childe Harold.* With Introduction and Notes, by H. F. TOZER, M.A. . . . . . [Extra fcap. 8vo, 3s. 6d. *In Parchment*, 5s.

Shelley. *Adonais.* With Introduction and Notes. By W. M. ROSSETTI. . . . . [Crown 8vo, 5s.

Scott. *Lady of the Lake.* Edited, with Preface and Notes, by W. MINTO, M.A. With Map. . . . [Extra fcap. 8vo, 3s. 6d.

———— *Lord of the Isles.* Edited, with Introduction and Notes, by THOMAS BAYNE . . . . [Extra fcap. 8vo, 3s. 6d.

———— *Lay of the Last Minstrel.* Edited by W. MINTO, M.A. With Map. . . . [Extra fcap. 8vo, *stiff covers*, 2s. *In Parchment*, 3s. 6d.

———— *Lay of the Last Minstrel.* Introduction and Canto I, with Preface and Notes, by W. MINTO, M.A. . . . . [*Paper covers*, 6d.

———— *Marmion.* Edited by T. BAYNE. . [Extra fcap. 8vo, 3s. 6d.

Campbell. *Gertrude of Wyoming.* Edited, with Introduction and Notes, by H. MACAULAY FITZGIBBON, M.A. *Second Edition* : [Extra fcap. 8vo, 1s.

Wordsworth. *The White Doe of Rylstone.* Edited by WILLIAM KNIGHT, LL.D., University of St. Andrews. . . [Extra fcap. 8vo, 2s. 6d.

Typical Selections *from the best English Writers. Second Edition.* In Two Volumes. . . . . . . [Extra fcap. 8vo, 3s. 6d. each.

HISTORY AND GEOGRAPHY, &c.

Freeman. *A Short History of the Norman Conquest of England.* By E. A. FREEMAN, M.A. *Second Edition.* . . [Extra fcap. 8vo, 2s. 6d.

Greswell. *History of the Dominion of Canada.* By W. PARR GRESWELL, M.A. . . . . [Crown 8vo, 7s. 6d.

———— *Geography of the Dominion of Canada and Newfoundland.* By the same Author. . . . . [Crown 8vo, 6s.

———— *Geography of Africa South of the Zambesi.* By the same Author. With Maps. . . . . . . [Crown 8vo, 7s. 6d.

Hughes (Alfred). *Geography for Schools.* Part I, *Practical Geography.* With Diagrams. . . . . [Extra fcap. 8vo, 2s. 6d.

Kitchin. *A History of France.* With Numerous Maps, Plans, and Tables. By G. W. KITCHIN, D.D., Dean of Winchester. *Second Edition.* Vol. I. To 1453. Vol. II. 1453–1624. Vol. III. 1624–1793. Each 10s. 6d.

Lucas. *Introduction to a Historical Geography of the British Colonies.* By C. P. LUCAS, B.A. . . . . [Crown 8vo, with 8 maps, 4s. 6d.

———— *Historical Geography of the British Colonies:*—

    I. *The Mediterranean and Eastern Colonies* (exclusive of India).
[Crown 8vo, with 11 maps, 5s.

    II. *The West Indian Dependencies.* With Twelve Maps.
[Crown 8vo, 7s. 6d.

MATHEMATICS AND PHYSICAL SCIENCE.

Aldis. *A Text Book of Algebra (with Answers to the Examples).* By W. Steadman Aldis, M.A. . . . . . . [Crown 8vo, 7s. 6d.

Hamilton and **Ball.** *Book-keeping.* By Sir R. G. C. Hamilton, K.C.B., and John Ball (of the firm of Quilter, Ball, & Co.). *New and Enlarged Edition.* . . . . [Extra fcap. 8vo, 2s.
*** *Ruled Exercise Books adapted to the above;* fcap. folio, 1s. 6d. *Ruled Book adapted to the Preliminary Course;* small 4to, 4d.

Hensley. *Figures made Easy: a first Arithmetic Book.* By Lewis Hensley, M.A. . . . . [Crown 8vo, 6d.

———— *Answers to the Examples in Figures made Easy.* By the same Author. . . . . [Crown 8vo, 1s.

———— *The Scholar's Arithmetic.* By the same Author.
[Crown 8vo, 2s. 6d.

———— *Answers to the Examples in the Scholar's Arithmetic.* By the same Author. . . . . [Crown 8vo, 1s. 6d.

———— *The Scholar's Algebra.* An Introductory work on Algebra. By the same Author. . . . . . . [Crown 8vo, 2s. 6d.

Minchin. *Hydrostatics and Elementary Hydrokinetics.* By G. M. Minchin, M.A. . . . . [Crown 8vo, 10s. 6d.

Selby. *Elementary Mechanics of Solids and Fluids.* By A. L. Selby, M.A. . . . . [Crown 8vo, 7s. 6d.

Nixon. *Euclid Revised.* Containing the essentials of the Elements of Plane Geometry as given by Euclid in his First Six Books. Edited by R. C. J. Nixon. M.A. *Second Edition.* . . . . . [Crown 8vo, 6s.
May likewise be had in parts as follows :—
Book I, 1s.   Books I, II, 1s. 6d.   Books I-IV, 3s.   Books V, VI, 3s.

———— *Supplement to Euclid Revised.* By the same Author. [*Stiff,* 6d.

———— *Geometry in Space.* Containing parts of Euclid's Eleventh and Twelfth Books. By the same Author. . . . [Crown 8vo, 3s. 6d.

———— *Elementary Plane Trigonometry; that is, Plane Trigonometry without Imaginaries.* By the same Author . . . [Crown 8vo, 7s. 6d.

Fisher. *Class-Book of Chemistry.* By W. W. Fisher, M.A., F.C.S. *Second Edition* . . . . [Crown 8vo, 4s. 6d.

Harcourt and **Madan.** *Exercises in Practical Chemistry.* Vol. I. *Elementary Exercises.* By A. G. Vernon Harcourt, M.A., and H. G. Madan, M.A. *Fourth Edition.* Revised by H. G. Madan, M.A.
[Crown 8vo, 10s. 6d.

Williamson. *Chemistry for Students.* By A. W. Williamson, Phil. Doc., F.R.S. . . . . [Extra fcap. 8vo, 8s. 6d.

Fowler. *The Elements of Deductive Logic,* designed mainly for the use of Junior Students in the Universities. By T. Fowler, D.D. *Ninth Edition,* with a Collection of Examples. [Extra fcap. 8vo, 3s. 6d.

——— *The Elements of Inductive Logic,* designed mainly for the use of Students in the Universities. *Fifth Edition.* [Extra fcap. 8vo, 6s.

Music.—Farmer. *Hymns and Chorales for Schools and Colleges.* Edited by John Farmer. Organist of Balliol College. . . . . [5s.
☞ *Hymns without the Tunes,* 2s.

Hullah. *The Cultivation of the Speaking Voice.* By John Hullah. [Extra fcap. 8vo, 2s. 6d.

Maclaren. *A System of Physical Education: Theoretical and Practical.* With 346 Illustrations drawn by A. Macdonald, of the Oxford School of Art. By Archibald Maclaren, the Gymnasium, Oxford. *Second Edition.* [Extra fcap. 8vo, 7s. 6d.

Troutbeck and Dale. *A Music Primer for Schools.* By J. Troutbeck, D.D., formerly Music Master in Westminster School, and R. F. Dale, M.A., B.Mus., late Assistant Master in Westminster School. [Crown 8vo, 1s. 6d.

Tyrwhitt. *A Handbook of Pictorial Art.* By R. St. J. Tyrwhitt, M.A. With coloured Illustrations, Photographs, and a chapter on Perspective, by A. Macdonald. *Second Edition.* . . . [8vo, *half-morocco,* 18s.

Upcott. *An Introduction to Greek Sculpture.* By L. E. Upcott, M.A. . . . . [Crown 8vo, 4s. 6d.

Student's Handbook to the University and Colleges of Oxford. *Twelfth Edition.* . . . . [Crown 8vo, 2s. 6d.

Helps to the Study of the Bible, taken from the *Oxford Bible for Teachers.* A new, enlarged, and illustrated edition, comprising Introductions to the several Books, the History and Antiquities of the Jews, the results of Modern Discoveries, and the Natural History of Palestine, with copious Tables, Concordance and Indices, and a series of Maps. . . [Crown 8vo, 4s. 6d.

Helps to the Study of the Book of Common Prayer. Being a Companion to Church Worship. . . . . . [Crown 8vo, 3s. 6d.

. A Reading Room *has been opened at the* Clarendon Press Warehouse, Amen Corner, *where visitors will find every facility for examining old and new works issued from the Press, and for consulting all official publications.*

London: HENRY FROWDE,
Oxford University Press Warehouse, Amen Corner.
Edinburgh: 12 Frederick Street.

LaVergne, TN USA
23 March 2011

221338LV00003B/117/P